READING RUTH: A GUIDE TO THE HEBREW TEXT

Charles L. Echols

Copyright © 2010 by Charles L. Echols

All rights reserved. No parts of this book may be reproduced, stored in a retrieval system, or transmitted in any form or by any means, electronic, mechanical, including photocopying, recording, or otherwise, without the written permission of the author.

Biblia Hebraica Stuttgartensia, © 1967/77 Deutsche Bibelgesellschaft. Used by permission. Unicode adaptation of *Biblia Hebraica Stuttgartensia*, © David Instone-Brewer. Used by permission.

ISBN 978-1-257-43785-6

CONTENTS

Preface v
Introduction vii
Chapter 1 1
Chapter 2 25
Chapter 3 43
Chapter 4 57
Appendices 71
    Translation 73
    Abbreviations 91
    Accents 95
    Basic Grammatical Terms 99

PREFACE

It is now rather common for people to pursue studies intermittently rather than continuously from start to finish. One might, for example, complete an undergraduate degree and return years later to pursue the subject at the postgraduate level. Similarly, a student might take an introductory course in a language, but not recommence further studies in it until a semester or more later. Usually in such cases, only vestiges of familiarity with the language remain.

This book is designed for those who have had an introductory course in Biblical Hebrew at some point in the past and wish to resume their study of the language. It is also written with awareness of the fact that such readers may not have access to an adequate library. Hence, the book provides everything necessary to read the book of Ruth in Hebrew, including the text, translation, and any pertinent grammatical and lexical information.

I want to emphasize that the focus is on reacquainting the reader with the basics of Hebrew grammar. Hence, not attention is given to critical aspects of the book of Ruth such as authorship, date, setting, purpose/occasion, and theology. Similarly, I have excluded discussion of textual criticism except with respect to יִגְאַל in 4:4. Moreover, intermediate and/or advanced grammatical and syntactical aspects of the Hebrew text are discussed only where a beginning Hebrew student would experience difficulty translating without an explanation.

I am indebted to Dr. Dale Brueggemann, who read the manuscript and made several useful suggestions, and to the Rev. Dr. Andrew Macintosh, with whom I consulted regarding an aspect of Kethiv/Qere and the pointing of בָּאנָה in 1:19. I am also grateful to three of my students, Ms. Benrilo Kikon, Mr. Imlong Chang, and Mr. Janak B. C., who "road tested" parts of the manuscript. Any errors found in the manuscript are, however, solely mine. This book is dedicated with love to my wife, Janet.

April 2011
Union Biblical Seminary, Pune

INTRODUCTION

This book pursues an inductive approach towards reading the book of Ruth, with vocabulary and grammar introduced as they occur. Hence, the reader should begin at chapter one, verse one, and proceed in order. To develop reading facility, the Hebrew text should be read aloud before working through the grammar and translation. Because knowing the vocabulary is half the battle, it follows that any unknown words should be committed to memory as they arise.

For each verse the Hebrew text appears first, with the individual words of the verse appearing in order on the left margin. Each word in the margin is then parsed, and its lexical root is given in parentheses, followed by the English meaning of the word.[1] For example, in Ruth 1:4, נָשִׁים appears on the left margin, followed by the parsing (nfp), the lexical root in parentheses (אִשָּׁה), and finally the English translation of the word its lexical form, i.e., "woman." For verbs the English meaning given is the infinitive of the root

---

[1] If a word appears in its lexical form in the text (e.g., masculine singular nouns, or Qal suffixed third masculine singular verbs), the parsing does not repeat the form. Unless otherwise noted, the meanings supplied are those from BDB and *HALOT*.

in the particular stem. For example, again in 1:4, the value for וַיִּשְׂאוּ (a Qal pref 3mp) is "to lift, carry, take," based on the Qal stem נָשָׂא. The translations, however, reflect the meaning of the term in the context of the verse; hence, "women," for נָשִׁים, and "took" for וַיִּשְׂאוּ.

In order to bring the reader "up to speed," all words of every verse in chapter 1 are listed (unless a word occurs more than once in the same verse, in which case only the first occurrence appears). Thereafter, the general practice is to parse only new words or forms. Similarly, the English meaning of all prepositions is given only once, at the first occurrence of each preposition; but the reader can always refer to the translation at the end of the verse if s/he forgets the meaning subsequently.

To gain proficiency, one should try to translate each verse independently, and then check the translation in the appendix. The translation provided (the first appendix) is the author's, and tends towards formal rather than dynamic equivalency. Although this results in a translation that is somewhat awkward at points, the choice is intentional in order to reflect the Hebrew grammar more closely; and the reader is of course free to consult more the standard translations (e.g., NRSV, NAS, NIV). In many instances an English word must be supplied to the translation, in which case it appears in brackets (e.g., [was], 1:2).

Besides the translation, there are three other

Introduction

appendices. The first is a list of abbreviations used in the book, followed by a table of accents. I have found that many students have little knowledge of the basic parts of speech (e.g., subject, verb, object). An understanding of these building blocks of syntax is, however, essential for translating Hebrew (or any language). Hence, the final appendix is a list of basic grammatical terms.

CHAPTER 1

1:1
וַיְהִ֗י בִּימֵי֙ שְׁפֹ֣ט הַשֹּׁפְטִ֔ים וַיְהִ֥י רָעָ֖ב בָּאָ֑רֶץ וַיֵּ֨לֶךְ אִ֜ישׁ מִבֵּ֧ית לֶ֣חֶם יְהוּדָ֗ה לָגוּר֙ בִּשְׂדֵ֣י מוֹאָ֔ב ה֖וּא וְאִשְׁתּ֥וֹ וּשְׁנֵ֥י בָנָֽיו׃

וַיְהִי	Qal pret w/c 3ms (הָיָה), "to be." Although the verb can be translated variously (e.g., "And it came to pass . . ."), its main function is to begin a narrative of a past event. As such it may be omitted from the translation. Here, however, it initiates a dependent (temporal) clause, and can be translated as "when."
בִּימֵי	Prep (בְּ), "in, by, with, at among, on," + nmp con (יוֹם), "day."
שְׁפֹט	Qal inf con (שָׁפַט), "to judge."
הַשֹּׁפְטִים	Art + Qal act ptcp mp (שָׁפַט), "to judge."
וַיְהִי	Qal pret w/c 3ms. The conjunction introduces the main (declarative) clause, (i.e., "a famine was in the land"). Again, rather than translating, "and it came to

Reading Ruth

	pass," simply translating "there was" is customary (i.e., "there was a famine in the land").
רָעָב	Nms, "famine."
בָּאָרֶץ	Prep + art, "the," + nfs (אֶרֶץ), "earth."
וַיֵּלֶךְ	Qal pret w/c 3ms (הָלַךְ), "to walk, go." The conjunction begins a dependent (logical or inferential) clause.
אִישׁ	Nms, "man."
מִבֵּית לֶחֶם	Prep (מִן), "from," + npr, "Bethlehem."
יְהוּדָה	Npr, "Judah."
לָגוּר	Prep, "to, towards, until, for," + Qal inf con, "to sojourn."
בִּשְׂדֵי	Prep + nmp con (שָׂדֶה), "field, country." The word could be translated "fields" as in "fields of Moab," but the more common rendering uses the singular "country."
מוֹאָב	Npr, "Moab."
הוּא	Pron ip 3ms, "he, it."
וְאִשְׁתּוֹ	Conj, "and," + nfs con (אִשָּׁה), "woman, wife," + 3ms ps.
וּשְׁנֵי	Conj + adj m du con (שְׁנַיִם), "two."
בָנָיו	Nmp con (בֵּן), "son," + 3ms ps.

1:2

וְשֵׁם הָאִישׁ אֱלִימֶלֶךְ וְשֵׁם אִשְׁתּוֹ נָעֳמִי וְשֵׁם שְׁנֵי־בָנָיו מַחְלוֹן וְכִלְיוֹן אֶפְרָתִים מִבֵּית לֶחֶם יְהוּדָה וַיָּבֹאוּ שְׂדֵי־מוֹאָב וַיִּהְיוּ־שָׁם׃

CHAPTER 1

וְשֵׁם	Conj + nms con, "name." Since the absolute noun is definite (הָאִישׁ), the construct is also definite. The article should therefore be supplied ("*the* man"). The conjunction introduces a dependent (parenthetical) clause.
הָאִישׁ	Art + nms (see 1:1).
אֱלִימֶלֶךְ	Npr, "Elimelech."
אִשְׁתּוֹ	See 1:1.
נָעֳמִי	Npr, "Naomi."
שְׁנֵי	See 1:1.
בָנָיו	See 1:1.
מַחְלוֹן	Npr, "Mahlon."
וְכִלְיוֹן	Conj + npr, "Chilion."
אֶפְרָתִים	Adj prg (אֶפְרָתִי), "Ephrathites." The phrase אֶפְרָתִים מִבֵּית לֶחֶם יְהוּדָה is epexegetical to what precedes. In other words it gives more information about the family.
מִבֵּית לֶחֶם	See 1:1.
יְהוּדָה	See 1:1.
וַיָּבֹאוּ	Qal pret w/c 3mp (בּוֹא), "to come, go."
שְׂדֵי־מוֹאָב	See 1:1.
וַיִּהְיוּ	Qal pret w/c 3mp (הָיָה), "to go."
שָׁם	Adv, "there."

This verse has three noun clauses, that is, a subject and a predicate without a verb. With nominal sentences, the reader must supply the verb "to be" (הָיָה), or its equivalent based on whether the action, as determined by context, is present (e.g., "is," "are"), future (e.g., "will be"), or past (e.g., "was," "were"). In this book the verb of a noun sentence will be supplied in brackets.

1:3

וַיָּמָת אֱלִימֶלֶךְ אִישׁ נָעֳמִי וַתִּשָּׁאֵר הִיא וּשְׁנֵי בָנֶיהָ׃

וַיָּמָת	Qal pret w/c 3ms (מוּת), "to die." Sequence use of the conjunction, "then."
אֱלִימֶלֶךְ	See 1:2.
אִישׁ	See 1:1.
נָעֳמִי	See 1:2.
וַתִּשָּׁאֵר	Niph pret w/c 3fs (שָׁאַר), "to be left over or behind, remain, be left alive, survive. Logical use of the conjunction, "so."
הִיא	Pron ip 3fs, "she, it." Since the verb supplies the subject, the pronoun is emphatic, underscoring the isolation Naomi would have felt after Elimelech's death, even though her sons remained with her.
וּשְׁנֵי	See 1:1.
בָנֶיהָ	Nmp con (בֵּן), "son," + 3fs ps.

Chapter 1

1:4

וַיִּשְׂאוּ לָהֶם נָשִׁים מֹאֲבִיּוֹת שֵׁם הָאַחַת עָרְפָּה וְשֵׁם הַשֵּׁנִית רוּת וַיֵּשְׁבוּ שָׁם כְּעֶשֶׂר שָׁנִים׃

וַיִּשְׂאוּ	Qal pret w/c 3mp (נָשָׂא), "to lift, carry, take." In the prefixed conjugation, the initial *nûn* in I-Nûn verbs assimilates into the second radical. It is usually represented by a dagesh forte; but if the radical has a shewa, the dagesh is often omitted (see *GBH*, §§18m, 19).
לָהֶם	Prep + 3mp ps (reflexive), "for themselves."
נָשִׁים	Nfp (אִשָּׁה), "woman."
מֹאֲבִיּוֹת	Adj g (מוֹאָבִי, מוֹאֲבִיָּה), "Moabite."
שֵׁם	See 1:2.
הָאַחַת	Art + adj fs (אֶחָד), "one."
עָרְפָּה	Npr, "Orpah."
וְשֵׁם	Conj + nms con (see 1:2).
הַשֵּׁנִית	Art + adj fs (שֵׁנִי), "second," but with אֶחָד = "other."
רוּת	Npr, "Ruth."
וַיֵּשְׁבוּ	Qal pret w/c 3mp (יָשַׁב), "to sit, wait, remain, dwell, live."
שָׁם	Adv, "there."
כְּעֶשֶׂר	Prep, "like, as, as many, about, according to," + adj fs, "ten."
שָׁנִים	Nfp (שָׁנָה), "year."

1:5

וַיָּמוּתוּ גַם־שְׁנֵיהֶם מַחְלוֹן וְכִלְיוֹן וַתִּשָּׁאֵר הָאִשָּׁה מִשְּׁנֵי יְלָדֶיהָ וּמֵאִישָׁהּ:

וַיָּמוּתוּ	Qal pret w/c 3mp (מות), "to die."
גַם	Adv, "also, both, as well as, even."
שְׁנֵיהֶם	Adj m du con (שְׁנַיִם), "two," + 3mp ps, "them."
מַחְלוֹן	See 1:2.
וְכִלְיוֹן	See 1:2.
וַתִּשָּׁאֵר	Niph pret w/c 3fs (שָׁאַר), "to remain, be left over." The conjunction translates as "so that," and initiates a dependent (result) clause.
הָאִשָּׁה	Art + nfs, "woman, wife, female."
מִשְּׁנֵי	Prep (מִן), "from, of," + adj m du con (שְׁנַיִם), "two."
יְלָדֶיהָ	Nmp con (יֶלֶד), "child, son, boy, youth," + 3fs ps, "her."
וּמֵאִישָׁהּ	Conj, "and," + prep + nms con, "man," + 3fs ps, "her."

1:6

וַתָּקָם הִיא וְכַלֹּתֶיהָ וַתָּשָׁב מִשְּׂדֵי מוֹאָב כִּי שָׁמְעָה בִּשְׂדֵה מוֹאָב כִּי־פָקַד יְהוָה אֶת־עַמּוֹ לָתֵת לָהֶם לָחֶם:

וַתָּקָם	Qal pret w/c 3fs (קום), "to rise, stand." The *wāw* conjunction is sequential,

Chapter 1

"then."

הִיא — Pron ip 3fs, "she, it." With a verb that indicates the subject (i.e., וַתָּקָם), the pronoun is emphatic ("herself"), here to distinguish the principal character of the verse.

וְכַלֹּתֶיהָ — Conj + nfp con (כַּלָּה), "daughter-in-law, bride," + 3fs ps. The *wāw* is accompaniment, "with."

וַתָּשָׁב — Qal pret w/c 3fs (שׁוּב), "turn back, return." The form of the verb here and in v. 22 is slightly different than the standard, וַתֵּשֶׁב, as in 2:14, 23.

מִשְּׂדֵי — Prep + nmp con (שָׂדֶה), "field, country."

מוֹאָב — Npr, "Moab."

כִּי — Conj, "that, for, because, when."

שָׁמְעָה — Qal suff 3fs (שָׁמַע), "to hear."

פָּקַד — Qal suff 3ms, "to visit, attend to, appoint, muster."

יְהוָה — Npr, "YHWH," "Yahweh," or "the LORD."

אֶת — Sign of the accusative.

עַמּוֹ — Nms con (עַם), "people, nation," + 3ms ps.

לָתֵת — Prep + Qal inf con (נָתַן), "to give, put, set."

לָהֶם — Prep (לְ) + 3mp ps (הֵם).

לָחֶם — Nms (in pause; lexical form is לֶחֶם), "bread, food."

1:7

וַתֵּצֵא מִן־הַמָּקוֹם אֲשֶׁר הָיְתָה־שָּׁמָּה וּשְׁתֵּי כַלֹּתֶיהָ
עִמָּהּ וַתֵּלַכְנָה בַדֶּרֶךְ לָשׁוּב אֶל־אֶרֶץ יְהוּדָה:

וַתֵּצֵא	Qal pret w/c 2fs (יָצָא), "to come/go out."
מִן	Prep (see 1:1).
הַמָּקוֹם	Art + nms, "place."
אֲשֶׁר	Pron rel, "who, which, what, where."
הָיְתָה	Qal suff 3fs (הָיָה), "to be."
שָׁמָּה	Adv, "there," + directive *hē*.
וּשְׁתֵּי	Conj + adj f du con (שְׁנַיִם; see 1:1).
כַלֹּתֶיהָ	See 1:6.
עִמָּהּ	Prep (עִם), "with," + 3fs ps.
וַתֵּלַכְנָה	Qal pret w/c 3fp (הָלַךְ), "to come, go, walk."
בַדֶּרֶךְ	Prep + art + nm/fs, "way, road, distance, journey, manner."
לָשׁוּב	Prep + Qal inf con, "to return."
אֶל	Prep, "to, toward, into."
אֶרֶץ	Nfs, "land, earth."
יְהוּדָה	Npr, "Judah."

1:8

וַתֹּאמֶר נָעֳמִי לִשְׁתֵּי כַלֹּתֶיהָ לֵכְנָה שֹּׁבְנָה אִשָּׁה לְבֵית
אִמָּהּ [כ = יַעֲשֶׂה] יְהוָה עִמָּכֶם חֶסֶד כַּאֲשֶׁר עֲשִׂיתֶם
עִם־הַמֵּתִים וְעִמָּדִי:

וַתֹּאמֶר	Qal pret w/c 3fs (אָמַר), "to say."

Chapter 1

נָעֳמִי	See 1:2.
לִשְׁתֵּי	Prep + adj f du con (שְׁתַיִם, שְׁנַיִם), "two."
כַּלֹּתֶיהָ	See 1:6.
לֵכְנָה	Qal impv fp (הָלַךְ, see 1:7).
שֹׁבְנָה	Qal impv fp (שׁוּב, see 1:6).
אִשָּׁה	Nfs, "woman, wife," but here used distributively, "each of you."
לְבֵית	Prep + nms con (בַּיִת), "house."
אִמָּהּ	Nfs (אֵם), "mother," + 3fs ps.

INTRODUCING KETHIV/QERE

Kethiv, or "what is written" (from כָּתַב, "to write")
Qere, or "what is read" (from קָרָא, "to read")

The Hebrew text that we read is the final product of a group of Jews called the Masoretes, who, from ca. A.D. 800-1000, edited and passed on the Hebrew text that they had received. Their reverence for the received consonantal text was such that they made no changes to it. Instead, they added a system of vowels and notes in the text (e.g., vowel pointing) and in the outer and lower margins of the text (the *masora parvum* and *masora magnum*, respectively).

The system of Kethiv (כ)/Qere (ק) is an example of notation that the Masoretes used when they encountered a difference between the way that a word was written in the received text and the way that they pronounced it. In such instances, the Masoretes made no changes to the consonantal text (כ), but pointed the word in question according to their pronunciation and placed a small circle over it. The circle directed the reader to the *masora parvum*, where the Masoretes wrote what they regarded as the correct reading – the Qere.

Differences between the Kethiv and the Qere may result from textual corruption of the Kethiv, or they may simply reflect a different reading tradition than that of the Masoretes. In general, the Qere reading is to be followed, as is the case for all of the occurrences of Kethiv/Qere in the book of Ruth, except for 3:5 and 3:17. In this book, the text at the beginning of each verse shows the Kethiv as it appears in the Masoretic text, and the text in the left margin supplies the Kethiv again, this time with parsing (according to the consonantal text), followed by the Qere.

כ= יַעֲשֶׂה   Qal pref 3ms (עָשָׂה), "to do, make, work." The prefixed conjugation generally expresses the indicative (e.g., "Yahweh will . . ." or "Yahweh is going to . . ."), but it can express modality (cf. *GBH*, §113l).

ק= יַעַשׂ   Qal pref (juss) 3ms (עָשָׂה), "to do, make, work." The Masoretes understood

CHAPTER 1

	Naomi's speech to Orpah and Ruth as a blessing (i.e., "May Yahweh…"), hence the jussive.
יְהוָה	See 1:6.
עִמָּכֶם	Prep, usually "with," but as a "personal compliment with verbs" (*IBHS*, §11.2.14b), the meaning is "to," + 2mp ps.
חֶסֶד	Nms, "goodness, kindness."
כַּאֲשֶׁר	Prep + pron rel.
עֲשִׂיתֶם	Qal suff 2mp (עָשָׂה), see above.
עִם	Prep.
הַמֵּתִים	Art + Qal act ptcp mp (מוּת), "to die."
וְעִמָּדִי	Conj + prep (עִם) + 1cs ps. This form of the preposition with 1cs ps is anomalous (*IBHS*, §11.2.14a, *GBH*, §103i).

1:9

יִתֵּן יְהוָה לָכֶם וּמְצֶאןָ מְנוּחָה אִשָּׁה בֵּית אִישָׁהּ וַתִּשַּׁק לָהֶן וַתִּשֶּׂאנָה קוֹלָן וַתִּבְכֶּינָה׃

יִתֵּן	Qal juss (same form as prefixed) 3ms (נָתַן), "to give."
יְהוָה	See 1:6.
לָכֶם	Prep + 2mp ps.
וּמְצֶאןָ	Conj (purpose), "that," + Qal impv fp (מָצָא), "to attain to, find."
מְנוּחָה	Nfs, "resting place, rest."
אִשָּׁה	See 1:1, but here used distributively, i.e.

	"each of you" (cf. *GBH*, §147d).
בֵּית	See 1:8.
אִישָׁהּ	Nms con (אִישׁ, see 1:1), + 3fs ps.
וַתִּשַּׁק	Qal pret w/c 3fs (נָשַׁק), "to kiss."
לָהֶן	Prep + 3fp ps.
וַתִּשֶּׂאנָה	Qal pret w/c 3fp (נָשָׂא), "to lift, carry, take."
קוֹלָן	Nms con, "voice," + 3fp ps.
וַתִּבְכֶּינָה	Qal pret w/c 3fp (בָּכָה), "to weep."

1:10

וַתֹּאמַרְנָה־לָּהּ כִּי־אִתָּךְ נָשׁוּב לְעַמֵּךְ׃

וַתֹּאמַרְנָה	Qal pret w/c 3fp (אָמַר, see 1:8).
לָּהּ	Prep + 3fs ps.
כִּי	Conj (here having an intensive force), "surely" (s.v. I כִּי, 1.3, BDB).
אִתָּךְ	Prep (אֵת), "with," + 2fs ps.
נָשׁוּב	Qal pref 1cp (שׁוּב, see 1:6).
לְעַמֵּךְ	Prep + nms con (עַם, see 1:6) + 2fs ps.

1:11

וַתֹּאמֶר נָעֳמִי שֹׁבְנָה בְנֹתַי לָמָּה תֵלַכְנָה עִמִּי הַעוֹד־לִי בָנִים בְּמֵעַי וְהָיוּ לָכֶם לַאֲנָשִׁים׃

וַתֹּאמֶר	See 1:8. Conjunction is adversative, "but."
נָעֳמִי	See 1:2.
שֹׁבְנָה	See 1:8.

Chapter 1

בְּנֹתַי	Nfp con (בַּת), "daughter," + 1cs ps.
לָמָּה	Prep + pron inter, "why?"
תֵלַכְנָה	Qal pref 2fp (הָלַךְ, see 1:1).
עִמִּי	Prep (see 1:7) + 1cs ps.
הַעוֹד	Ptcl interrog (the normal pointing with *ḥāṭēp-pátaḥ* changes to *pátaḥ* before ע) + adv, "still, yet, again, besides." The interrogative particle initiates a rhetorical question.
לִי	Prep + 1cs ps.
בָנִים	Nmp (בֵּן, see 1:1).
בְמֵעַי	Prep + nmp con (מֵעֶה), "womb, belly, internal organs," + 1cs ps.
וְהָיוּ	Qal suff w/c 3cp (הָיָה, see 1:1). The *wāw* denotes purpose, "that."
לָכֶם	Prep + 2mp ps.
לַאֲנָשִׁים	Prep + nmp (אִישׁ, see 1:1).

1:12

שֹׁבְנָה בְנֹתַי לֵכְןָ כִּי זָקַנְתִּי מִהְיוֹת לְאִישׁ כִּי אָמַרְתִּי יֶשׁ־לִי תִקְוָה גַּם הָיִיתִי הַלַּיְלָה לְאִישׁ וְגַם יָלַדְתִּי בָנִים׃

שֹׁבְנָה	See 1:8.
בְנֹתַי	See 1:11.
לֵכְןָ	Qal impv fp (הָלַךְ, see 1:1).
כִּי	Conj, "for, because."
זָקַנְתִּי	Qal suff 1cs (זָקֵן), "to be/become old."
מִהְיוֹת	Prep (מִן, comparative), "too," + Qal inf

	con (הָיָה, see 1:1).
לְאִישׁ	Prep + nms (see 1:1).
כִּי	Conj, which translates as "if," and initiates a dependent (conditional) clause.
אָמַרְתִּי	Qal suff 1cs (אָמַר, see 1:8).
יֵשׁ	Ptcl of being (יֵשׁ), substance, existence, usually "there is," but with the following לִי, "I have."
לִי	See 1:11.
תִקְוָה	Nfs, "hope."
גַּם	See 1:5.
הָיִיתִי	Qal suff 1cs (הָיָה, see 1:1).
הַלַּיְלָה	Art, functioning as demonstrative adj, "this," + nms, "night."
יָלַדְתִּי	Qal suff 1cs (יָלַד, see 1:5). Strictly speaking, the suffixed conjugation does not express moods such as the subjunctive, as is translated here, i.e., "should bear…" Yet, if it is preceded by a hypothetical particle, in this case גַּם, then a subjunctive nuance is possible (cf. *IBHS*, §30.5.4ab).
בָנִים	See 1:11.

1:13

הֲלָהֵן ׀ תְּשַׂבֵּרְנָה עַד אֲשֶׁר יִגְדָּלוּ הֲלָהֵן תֵּעָגֵנָה לְבִלְתִּי הֱיוֹת לְאִישׁ אַל בְּנֹתַי כִּי־מַר־לִי מְאֹד מִכֶּם כִּי־יָצְאָה בִי יַד־יְהוָה׃

CHAPTER 1

הֲלָהֵן	Ptcl interrog, "why," + conj, "on this account, therefore."
תְּשַׂבֵּרְנָה	Piel pref 2fp (שָׂבַר), "to wait, hope," with volative nuance, "would."
עַד אֲשֶׁר	Prep, "as far as, until, even to, while," + pron rel (see 1:7) = "until" (s.v. III עַד, B.b, *HALOT*).
יִגְדָּלוּ	Qal pref 3mp (גָּדַל), "to grow up, become great."
תֵּעָגֵנָה	Niph pref 2fp (עָגַן), "to shut oneself in/off, let oneself be hindered from marriage," with volative nuance, "would."
לְבִלְתִּי	Ptcl neg used with the inf con.
הֱיוֹת	Qal inf con (הָיָה, see 1:1).
לְאִישׁ	See 1:12.
אַל	Ptcl neg used with cohortative and jussive. Here the particle conveys the (negative) answer to the previous question, the jussive being understood (*GBH*, §160.i.3).
בְּנֹתַי	See 1:11.
כִּי	See 1:6.
מַר	Qal suff 3ms (מָרַר), "to be bitter." Geminate verbs (verbs whose second and third radicals are the same) sometimes lose the third radical, and are pointed with a single *pataḥ*.
לִי	See 1:11.

מְאֹד	Adv, "much, greatly."
מִכֶּם	Prep (מִן) + 2mp ps. This is another instance of the comparative מִן, this time denoting a comparison of superiority or inferiority between two things. In this verse, Naomi states that her bitterness is more than that of her daughters-in-law. Hence, supply "more" and "than" accordingly.
יָצְאָה	Qal suff 3fs (יָצָא, see 1:7).
בִי	Prep (adversative), "against," + 1cs ps.
יַד	Nfs con (יָד), "hand."
יְהוָה	See 1:6.

1:14

וַתִּשֶּׂנָה קוֹלָן וַתִּבְכֶּינָה עוֹד וַתִּשַּׁק עָרְפָּה לַחֲמוֹתָהּ וְרוּת דָּבְקָה בָּהּ:

וַתִּשֶּׂנָה	Qal pret w/c 3fp (נָשָׂא), "to lift, carry, take away."
קוֹלָן	See 1:9.
וַתִּבְכֶּינָה	See 1:9.
עוֹד	Adv (see 1:11).
וַתִּשַּׁק	See 1:9.
עָרְפָּה	See 1:4.
לַחֲמוֹתָהּ	Prep + nfs con (חָמוֹת), "husband's mother," + 3fs ps.
וְרוּת	Conj (adversative), "but," + np (see 1:4).
דָּבְקָה	Qal suff 3fs (דָּבַק), "to cling, cleave."

Chapter 1

בָּהּ	Prep + 3fs ps.

1:15

וַתֹּאמֶר הִנֵּה שָׁבָה יְבִמְתֵּךְ אֶל־עַמָּהּ וְאֶל־אֱלֹהֶיהָ שׁוּבִי אַחֲרֵי יְבִמְתֵּךְ:

וַתֹּאמֶר	See 1:8.
הִנֵּה	Adv, "lo, see, behold!"
שָׁבָה	Qal suff 3fs (שׁוּב, see 1:6).
יְבִמְתֵּךְ	Nfs con (יְבָמָה), "sister-in-law," + 2fs ps.
אֶל	Prep.
עַמָּהּ	Nms con (עַם, see 1:6) + 3fs ps.
אֱלֹהֶיהָ	Nmp con (אֱלֹהִים), "gods, God," + 3fs ps.
שׁוּבִי	Qal impv fs (שׁוּב, see 1:6).
אַחֲרֵי	Adv. "behind, after."

1:16

וַתֹּאמֶר רוּת אַל־תִּפְגְּעִי־בִי לְעָזְבֵךְ לָשׁוּב מֵאַחֲרָיִךְ כִּי אֶל־אֲשֶׁר תֵּלְכִי אֵלֵךְ וּבַאֲשֶׁר תָּלִינִי אָלִין עַמֵּךְ עַמִּי וֵאלֹהַיִךְ אֱלֹהָי:

וַתֹּאמֶר	See 1:8.
רוּת	See 1:4.
אַל	See 1:13.
תִּפְגְּעִי	Qal pref (juss) 2fs (פָּגַע), "to meet, encounter, reach; request, entreat."
בִי	Prep + 1cs ps.

לְעָזְבֵךְ	Prep + Qal inf con (עָזַב), "to leave, forsake, loose," + 2fs ps.
לָשׁוּב	Prep + Qal inf con (שׁוּב, see 1:6).
מֵאַחֲרָיִךְ	Prep (מִן) + adv (see 1:15) + 2fs ps.
כִּי	Conj (see 1:6).
אֶל	Prep.
אֲשֶׁר	Pron rel (see 1:7).
תֵּלְכִי	Qal pref 2fs (הָלַךְ, see 1:1).
אֵלֵךְ	Qal pref 1cs.
וּבַאֲשֶׁר	Conj + prep + pron rel.
תָּלִינִי	Qal pref 2fs (לוּן/לִין), "to lodge, pass the night; fig. abide/live."
אָלִין	Qal pref 1cs (לוּן/לִין).
עַמֵּךְ	Nms con (עַם, see 1:6) + 2fs ps.
עַמִּי	Nms con, "people, nation," + 1cs ps.
וֵאלֹהַיִךְ	Conj + nmp con (see 1:15) + 2fs ps.
אֱלֹהָי	Nmp con (see 1:15) + 1cs ps. אֱלֹהִים can be translated in several ways. As in the previous verse, it can mean "gods." Here it is the so-called plural of majesty, and denotes the proper noun "God."

1:17

בַּאֲשֶׁר תָּמוּתִי אָמוּת וְשָׁם אֶקָּבֵר כֹּה יַעֲשֶׂה יְהוָה לִי וְכֹה יֹסִיף כִּי הַמָּוֶת יַפְרִיד בֵּינִי וּבֵינֵךְ:

בַּאֲשֶׁר	Prep + pron rel.
תָּמוּתִי	Qal pref 2fs (מוּת, see 1:3).

Chapter 1

אָמוּת	Qal pref 1cs.
וְשָׁם	Conj + adv, "there."
אֶקָּבֵר	Niph pref 1cs (קָבַר), "to bury."
כֹּה	Adv, "thus."
יַעֲשֶׂה	See 1:8.
יְהוָה	See 1:6.
לִי	See 1:11.
יֹסִיף	Hiph pref 3ms (יָסַף), "to add, increase; do again."
כִּי	Conj (here conditional), "if" (as in 1:12).
הַמָּוֶת	Art, used generically with an abstract state so that it is untranslated (see *IBHS*, §13.5.1.g) + nms (מָוֶת), "death."
יַפְרִיד	Hiph pref (juss) 3ms (פָּרַד), "to divide, separate."
בֵּינִי	Prep (בַּיִן), "between," + 1cs ps.
וּבֵינֵךְ	Conj + prep (בַּיִן) + 2fs ps.

1:18

וַתֵּרֶא כִּי־מִתְאַמֶּצֶת הִיא לָלֶכֶת אִתָּהּ וַתֶּחְדַּל לְדַבֵּר אֵלֶיהָ:

וַתֵּרֶא	Qal pret w/c 3fs (רָאָה), "to see." The conjunction, translated "when," initiates a dependent (temporal) clause.
כִּי	Conj.
מִתְאַמֶּצֶת	Hith act ptcp fs (אָמֵץ), "to strengthen oneself, be determined."
הִיא	See 1:3.

לָלֶכֶת	Prep + Qal inf con (הָלַךְ, see 1:1).
אִתָּהּ	Prep (see 1:10) + 3fs ps.
וַתֶּחְדַּל	Qal pret w/c 3fs (חָדַל), "to cease, leave off." The *wāw* conjunction, which can be translated as "then" or omitted, introduces the main clause.
לְדַבֵּר	Prep + Piel inf con (דָּבַר), "to speak."
אֵלֶיהָ	Prep + 3fs ps.

1:19

וַתֵּלַכְנָה שְׁתֵּיהֶם עַד־בֹּאָנָה בֵּית לָחֶם וַיְהִי כְּבֹאָנָה בֵּית לֶחֶם וַתֵּהֹם כָּל־הָעִיר עֲלֵיהֶן וַתֹּאמַרְנָה הֲזֹאת נָעֳמִי׃

וַתֵּלַכְנָה	Qal pret w/c 3fp (הָלַךְ, see 1:1).
שְׁתֵּיהֶם	Adj f du con (שְׁנַיִם; see 1:1) + 3mp ps.
עַד	See 1:13.
בֹּאָנָה	Qal inf con (בֹּא, see 1:2) + 3fp. The normal 3fp ps is ־ָן. The form here is rare, and perhaps for easier vocalization (*GBH*, §94h).
בֵּית לֶחֶם	See 1:1.
וַיְהִי	See 1:1.
כְּבֹאָנָה	Prep + Qal inf con (בֹּא, see 1:2) + 3fp ps.
וַתֵּהֹם	Niph pret w/c 3fs (הִים/הוּם), "to murmur, roar, discomfit."
כָּל	Nms con (כֹּל), "all, each, the whole, any."

CHAPTER 1

הָעִיר	Art + nms, "city."
עֲלֵיהֶן	Prep (עַל), "on, all, over, because of," + 3fp ps.
וַתֹּאמַרְנָה	See 1:10.
הֲזֹאת	Ptcl interrog + pron dem fs, "this."
נָעֳמִי	See 1:2.

1:20

וַתֹּאמֶר אֲלֵיהֶן אַל־תִּקְרֶאנָה לִי נָעֳמִי קְרֶאןָ לִי מָרָא כִּי־הֵמַר שַׁדַּי לִי מְאֹד:

וַתֹּאמֶר	See 1:8.
אֲלֵיהֶן	Prep + 3fp ps.
אַל	See 1:16.
תִּקְרֶאנָה	Qal pref 2fp (קָרָא), "to call, proclaim, name."
לִי	See 1:11.
נָעֳמִי	See 1:2.
קְרֶאןָ	Qal impv fp, apocopated *hē'* (cf. קְרֶאנָה*).
מָרָא	Adj fs, "bitter."
כִּי	See 1:6.
הֵמַר	Hiph suff 3ms (מָרַר), "to make bitter; to cause bitterness, grief.
שַׁדַּי	Nmp, but used as an appellative for God, usually rendered "the Almighty."
מְאֹד	See 1:13.

1:21

אֲנִי מְלֵאָה הָלַכְתִּי וְרֵיקָם הֱשִׁיבַנִי יְהוָה לָמָּה
תִקְרֶאנָה לִי נָעֳמִי וַיהוָה עָנָה בִי וְשַׁדַּי הֵרַע לִי:

אֲנִי	Pron ip 1cs.
מְלֵאָה	Adj fs (מָלֵא), "full."
הָלַכְתִּי	Qal suff 1cs (הָלַךְ, see 1:1).
וְרֵיקָם	Conj + adv, "emptily, vainly."
הֱשִׁיבַנִי	Hiph suff 1cs (שׁוּב), "to bring back, restore."
יְהוָה	See 1:6.
לָמָּה	See 1:11.
תִקְרֶאנָה	See 1:20.
לִי	See 1:11.
נָעֳמִי	See 1:2.
וַיהוָה	Conj + npr (see 1:6).
עָנָה	Qal suff 3ms, "to respond, answer; afflict."
בִי	See 1:13. Adversative use of the preposition.
וְשַׁדַּי	Conj (emotion), "Indeed!" (cf. *GBH*, §177m) + nmp (see 1:20).
הֵרַע	Hiph suff 3ms (רָעַע), "to do injury, hurt; do evil, wickedly; treat badly."

1:22

וַתָּשָׁב נָעֳמִי וְרוּת הַמּוֹאֲבִיָּה כַלָּתָהּ עִמָּהּ הַשָּׁבָה
מִשְּׂדֵי מוֹאָב וְהֵמָּה בָּאוּ בֵּית לֶחֶם בִּתְחִלַּת קְצִיר
שְׂעֹרִים:

CHAPTER 1

וַתָּשָׁב	See 1:6. Logical use of the conjunction, "thus, so."
נָעֳמִי	See 1:2.
וְרוּת	Conj + npr (See 1:4).
הַמּוֹאֲבִיָּה	Art + adj g (מוֹאָבִי), "Moabitess."
כַּלָּתָהּ	See 1:6.
עִמָּהּ	See 1:7.
הַשָּׁבָה	This form might be parsed as art (functioning as pron rel, "who") + Qal suff 3fs (שׁוּב, see 1:6), but more probably it is art + Qal act ptcp that was pointed as a Qal suff by the Masoretes (so *GBH*, §145i).
מִשְּׂדֵי מוֹאָב	See 1:6.
וְהֵמָּה	Conj + pron ip 3mp.
בָּאוּ	Qal suff 3cp (בּוֹא, see 1:2).
בֵּית לֶחֶם	See 1:1.
בִּתְחִלַּת	Prep (temporal), "in, at," + nfs con (תְּחִלָּה), "beginning."
קְצִיר	Nms con (קָצִיר), "harvest."
שְׂעֹרִים	Nfp (שְׂעֹרָה), "barley."

CHAPTER 2

2:1

וּלְנָעֳמִ֣י [כ= מְיֻדָּע] לְאִישָׁ֗הּ אִ֚ישׁ גִּבּ֣וֹר חַ֔יִל מִמִּשְׁפַּ֖חַת אֱלִימֶ֑לֶךְ וּשְׁמ֖וֹ בֹּֽעַז׃

וּלְנָעֳמִי	Conj + prep (possession) + npr.
כ= מְיֻדָּע	Pual ptcp ms (יָדַע), "to be known; acquaintance." Although the Pual participle of ידע occurs six times elsewhere in the OT, it is rare; and most read with the Qere here.
ק= מוֹדַע	Nms, "kinsman."
לְאִישָׁהּ	Prep + nms con (see 1:1) + 3fs ps.
גִּבּוֹר	Adj ms con, "strong, mighty, valiant."
חַיִל	Nms, "strength, efficiency, wealth, army."
מִמִּשְׁפַּחַת	Prep + nfs con (מִשְׁפָּחָה), "clan."
וּשְׁמוֹ	Conj + nms con (see 1:2) + 3ms ps.
בֹּעַז	Npr, "Boaz."

2:2

וַתֹּאמֶר֩ ר֨וּת הַמּוֹאֲבִיָּ֜ה אֶֽל־נָעֳמִ֗י אֵֽלְכָה־נָּ֤א הַשָּׂדֶה֙ וַאֲלַקֳטָ֣ה בַשִּׁבֳּלִ֔ים אַחַ֕ר אֲשֶׁ֥ר אֶמְצָא־חֵ֖ן בְּעֵינָ֑יו וַתֹּ֥אמֶר לָ֖הּ לְכִ֥י בִתִּֽי׃

הַמּוֹאֲבִיָּה	See 1:22.

אֵלְכָה־נָּא	Qal coh 1cs (הָלַךְ, see 1:1) + ptcl ent "please."
וַאֲלַקֳטָה	Conj + Piel coh 1cs (לָקַט), "to gather, pick, glean."
בַשִׁבֳּלִים	Prep + art + nfp (שִׁבֹּלֶת), "ear of grain."
אַחַר	Adv, "after."
אֶמְצָא	Qal pref 1cs (מָצָא), "to find." Although not a cohortative, the simple prefixed conjugation can express modality (*GBH,* §113l) as is the case here, "may."
חֵן	Nms, "grace, favor."
בְּעֵינָיו	Prep + nf du con (עַיִן), "eyes," + 3ms ps.
לְכִי	Qal impv fs (הָלַךְ, see 1:1).
בִּתִּי	Nfs con (בַּת, see 1:11).

2:3

וַתֵּלֶךְ וַתָּבוֹא וַתְּלַקֵּט בַּשָּׂדֶה אַחֲרֵי הַקֹּצְרִים וַיִּקֶר מִקְרֶהָ חֶלְקַת הַשָּׂדֶה לְבֹעַז אֲשֶׁר מִמִּשְׁפַּחַת אֱלִימֶלֶךְ׃

וַתֵּלֶךְ	Qal pret w/c 3fs.
וַתָּבוֹא	Qal pret w/c 3fs (בּוֹא; see 1:2).
וַתְּלַקֵּט	Piel pret w/c 3fs (see 2:2).
הַקֹּצְרִים	Art + Qal act ptcp mp (קָצַר), "to reap, harvest."
וַיִּקֶר	Qal pret w/c 3ms (קָרָה), "to encounter, meet, befall."
מִקְרֶהָ	Nfs con (מִקְרֶה), "accident, chance, fortune," + 3fs ps.
חֶלְקַת	Nfs con (חֶלְקָה), "portion."

Chapter 2

מִמִּשְׁפַּחַת אֱלִימֶלֶךְ   See 2:1.

2:4
וְהִנֵּה־בֹעַז בָּא מִבֵּית לֶחֶם וַיֹּאמֶר לַקּוֹצְרִים יְהוָה עִמָּכֶם וַיֹּאמְרוּ לוֹ יְבָרֶכְךָ יְהוָה:

וְהִנֵּה	Conj + adv (see 1:15).
בָּא	Qal act ptcp ms (בּוֹא), "to come."
וַיֹּאמֶר	Qal pret w/c 3ms (אָמַר; see 1:8).
לַקּוֹצְרִים	Prep + art + Qal act ptcp mp (see 2:3).
וַיֹּאמְרוּ	Qal pret w/c 3mp (אָמַר; see 1:8).
לוֹ	Prep + 3ms ps.
יְבָרֶכְךָ	Piel pref (juss) 3ms (בָּרַךְ), "to bless," + 2ms ps.

2:5
וַיֹּאמֶר בֹּעַז לְנַעֲרוֹ הַנִּצָּב עַל־הַקּוֹצְרִים לְמִי הַנַּעֲרָה הַזֹּאת:

לְנַעֲרוֹ	Prep + nms con (נַעַר), "boy, lad, young man; servant, retainer," + 3ms ps.
הַנִּצָּב	Art, functioning as the relative pronoun, "who," + Niph ptcp ms (נָצַב), "to station oneself, stand," here as a substantive ptcp, "deputy, prefect" as in a foreman.
עַל	Prep (see 1:19).
הַקּוֹצְרִים	See 2:3.
לְמִי	Prep + pron inter, "who?"

הַנַּעֲרָה	Art + nfs, "girl, young (marriageable) woman, maid, maidservant."
הַזֹּאת	Art + pron dem fs (see 1:19).

2:6

וַיַּעַן הַנַּעַר הַנִּצָּב עַל־הַקּוֹצְרִים וַיֹּאמַר נַעֲרָה מוֹאֲבִיָּה הִיא הַשָּׁבָה עִם־נָעֳמִי מִשְּׂדֵה מוֹאָב:

וַיַּעַן	Qal pret w/c 3ms (עָנָה; see 1:21).
הַנַּעַר	Art + nms (נַעַר; see 2:5).
הַנִּצָּב	See 2:5. Here the article functions as a relative pronoun, "who."
נַעֲרָה	Nfs (see 2:5).
מוֹאֲבִיָּה	Adj g (see 1:4), in apposition.
הַשָּׁבָה	See 1:22.

2:7

וַתֹּאמֶר אֲלַקֳטָה־נָּא וְאָסַפְתִּי בָעֳמָרִים אַחֲרֵי הַקּוֹצְרִים וַתָּבוֹא וַתַּעֲמוֹד מֵאָז הַבֹּקֶר וְעַד־עַתָּה זֶה שִׁבְתָּהּ הַבַּיִת מְעָט:

אֲלַקֳטָה־נָּא	Piel cohort 1cs + ptcl ent.
וְאָסַפְתִּי	Qal suff w/c 1cs (אָסַף), "to gather, remove."
בָעֳמָרִים	Prep + art + nmp (עֹמֶר), "sheaf."
אַחֲרֵי	See 1:15.
הַקּוֹצְרִים	See 2:5.
וַתָּבוֹא	See 2:3.
וַתַּעֲמוֹד	Qal pret w/c 3fs (עָמַד), "to stand, take

CHAPTER 2

	one's stand."
מֵאָז	Prep + adv, "then, at that time."
הַבֹּקֶר	Art + nms, "morning."
וְעַד־עַתָּה	Conj + prep + adv, "now."
זֶה	Pron dem ms, "this." זֶה + עַתָּה = "just now."
שִׁבְתָּהּ	Qal inf con (יָשַׁב; see 1:4) + 3fs ps.
הַבַּיִת	Art + nms, "house."
מְעָט	Adj ms, "a little, a few, fewness."

2:8

וַיֹּאמֶר בֹּעַז אֶל־רוּת הֲלוֹא שָׁמַעַתְּ בִּתִּי אַל־תֵּלְכִי לִלְקֹט בְּשָׂדֶה אַחֵר וְגַם לֹא תַעֲבוּרִי מִזֶּה וְכֹה תִדְבָּקִין עִם־נַעֲרֹתָי׃

הֲלוֹא	Ptcl interrog + ptcl neg (written fully).
שָׁמַעַתְּ	Qal suff 2fs (see 1:6). With הֲלוֹא the (interrogative) clause is, "Have you not heard?" However, the interrogative particle can be used asseveratively, so that it is possible to translate, "Listen closely!"
בִּתִּי	See 2:2.
אַל	See 1:13.
תֵּלְכִי	See 1:16.
לִלְקֹט	Prep + Qal inf con (see 2:2).
אַחֵר	See 2:2.
וְגַם	See 1:12.
לֹא	Ptcl neg (written defectively).

תַעֲבוּרִי	Qal pref 2fs (עָבַר), "to pass over, through, by, on."
מִזֶּה	Prep + pron dem ms, functioning as a substantial adj, "this one."
וְכֹה	See 1:17.
תִדְבָּקִין	Qal pref 2fs (see 1:14) + paragogic *nûn*.
עִם	See 1:7.
נַעֲרֹתָי	Nfp con (see 2:5) + 1cs ps.

2:9

עֵינַיִךְ בַּשָּׂדֶה אֲשֶׁר־יִקְצֹרוּן וְהָלַכְתְּ אַחֲרֵיהֶן הֲלוֹא צִוִּיתִי אֶת־הַנְּעָרִים לְבִלְתִּי נָגְעֵךְ וְצָמִת וְהָלַכְתְּ אֶל־הַכֵּלִים וְשָׁתִית מֵאֲשֶׁר יִשְׁאֲבוּן הַנְּעָרִים׃

עֵינַיִךְ	Nf du con (עַיִן; see 2:2) + 2fs ps.
אֲשֶׁר	See 1:7.
יִקְצֹרוּן	Qal pref 3mp + paragogic *nûn*.
וְהָלַכְתְּ	Qal suff w/c 2fs (see 1:21).
אַחֲרֵיהֶן	Adv + 3fp ps.
הֲלוֹא	See 2:8.
צִוִּיתִי	Piel suff 1cs (צָוָה), "to give charge to, command, order."
הַנְּעָרִים	Art + nmp (נַעַר; see 2:5).
לְבִלְתִּי	See 1:13.
נָגְעֵךְ	Qal inf con (נָגַע), "to touch, reach, strike," + 2fs ps.
וְצָמִת	Qal suff w/c 2fs (צָמֵא), "to be thirsty." The conjunction translates as "when," and initiates a dependent (temporal)

Chapter 2

וְהָלַכְתְּ	clause. Because א is silent, it is occasionally drops out (*GBH*, §78e). See 1:21. The *wāw* begins (i.e., "then go . . .") the main clause, but "then" is usually omitted from the translation (cf. 1:1).
אֶל	See 1:7.
הַכֵּלִים	Art + nmp (כְּלִי), "article, utensil, vessel."
וְשָׁתִית	Qal suff w/c 2fs (שָׁתָה), "to drink."
מֵאֲשֶׁר	Prep + pron rel.
יִשְׁאֲבוּן	Qal pref 3mp (שָׁאַב), "to draw water," + paragogic *nûn*.

2:10

וַתִּפֹּל עַל־פָּנֶיהָ וַתִּשְׁתַּחוּ אָרְצָה וַתֹּאמֶר אֵלָיו מַדּוּעַ מָצָאתִי חֵן בְּעֵינֶיךָ לְהַכִּירֵנִי וְאָנֹכִי נָכְרִיָּה׃

וַתִּפֹּל	Qal pret w/c 3fs (נָפַל), "to fall, lie."
עַל	See 2:5.
פָּנֶיהָ	Nmp con (פָּנֶה), "face," + 3fs ps.
וַתִּשְׁתַּחוּ	This form is a 3fs prefixed conjugation w/c + 3ms ps, but there are two possibilities for the stem. The traditional view is that it is a Hithpalel from the root שָׁחָה, with שׁ and ת changing positions (metathesis), and the ה of the stem dropping with the addition of the 3ms ps (the ה of III-ה verbs are

31

commonly lost with inflection). Alternatively, it could be a Hishtaphel from the root חוי, with prefix הִשְׁתּ– (-תִּשְׁתּ for pref 3fs). Either way, the meaning is "to prostrate oneself," often in the context of worship.

אַ֫רְצָה — Nfs, "earth, ground," + directive *hē*, "to."

אֵלָיו — Prep + 3ms ps.

מַדּ֫וּעַ — Adv inter, "why?"

מְצָ֫אתִי — Qal suff 1cs (מָצָא; see 1:9).

חֵן — See 2:2.

בְּעֵינֶ֫יךָ — Prep + nf du con (עַ֫יִן; see 2:2) + 2ms ps.

לְהַכִּירֵ֫נִי — Prep + Hiph inf con (נָכַר), "to regard, observe," + 1cs ps. Verbal use of the infinitive. The modal nuance ("should") is explainable perhaps from the nature of the infinitive construct itself (see *GBH*, §124s, t) and/or following the interrogative מַדּ֫וּעַ.

וְאָנֹכִי — Conj (causal use, "because, since") + pron ip 1cs.

נָכְרִיָּה — Adj fs (נָכְרִי), "foreign, alien."

2:11

וַיַּ֫עַן בֹּ֫עַז וַיֹּ֫אמֶר לָהּ הֻגֵּד הֻגַּד לִי כֹּל אֲשֶׁר־עָשִׂית אֶת־חֲמוֹתֵךְ אַחֲרֵי מוֹת אִישֵׁךְ וַתַּעַזְבִי אָבִיךְ וְאִמֵּךְ וְאֶ֫רֶץ מוֹלַדְתֵּךְ וַתֵּלְכִי אֶל־עַם אֲשֶׁר לֹא־יָדַ֫עַתְּ תְּמוֹל שִׁלְשֽׁוֹם:

Chapter 2

וַיַּעַן	See 2:6.
הַגֵּד	Hophal inf abs (נָגַד). The use here is suggestive of the perfective use of the absolute, e.g., "fully" (cf. *GBH,* §123l.1)
הֻגַּד	Hophal suff 3ms, "to be told, announced, reported."
כֹּל	See 1:19.
עָשִׂית	Qal suff 2fs (עָשָׂה; see 1:8).
חֲמוֹתֵךְ	Nfs con (חָמוֹת; see 1:14) + 2fs ps.
מוֹת	Nms con (מָוֶת), "death."
אִישֵׁךְ	Nms con (אִישׁ; see 1:1) + 2fs ps.
וַתַּעַזְבִי	Qal pret w/c 2fs (עָזַב; see 1:16). Conj is epexegetical, "how."
אָבִיךְ	Nms con (אָב), "father," + 2fs ps.
וְאִמֵּךְ	Conj + nfs con (אֵם; see 1:8) + 2fs ps.
מוֹלַדְתֵּךְ	Nfs con (מוֹלֶדֶת, מוֹלָדָה), "birth," + 2fs ps.
יָדַעַתְּ	Qal suff 2fs (יָדַע), "to know, learn of, perceive."
תְּמוֹל	Adv, "yesterday, recently, formerly," + שִׁלְשׁוֹם, adv, "three days ago" = "yesterday, the day before yesterday, previously."

2:12

יְשַׁלֵּם יְהוָה פָּעֳלֵךְ וּתְהִי מַשְׂכֻּרְתֵּךְ שְׁלֵמָה מֵעִם יְהוָה
אֱלֹהֵי יִשְׂרָאֵל אֲשֶׁר־בָּאת לַחֲסוֹת תַּחַת־כְּנָפָיו:

יְשַׁלֵּם	Piel pref (juss) 3ms (שָׁלַם), "restore,

פָּעֳלֵךְ	Nms con (פֹּעַל), "deed, work," + 2fs ps.
וּתְהִי	Conj + Qal juss 2fs (הָיָה; see 1:1).
מַשְׂכֻּרְתֵּךְ	Nfs con (מַשְׂכֹּרֶת), "wages," + 2fs ps.
שְׁלֵמָה	Adj fs (שָׁלֵם), "complete, full, safe, at peace."
מֵעִם	Prep + prep = "from."
אֱלֹהֵי	See 1:15.
בָּאת	Qal suff 2fs (בּוֹא; see 1:2).
לַחֲסוֹת	Prep + Qal inf con (חָסָה), "to seek refuge."
תַּחַת	Prep, "under, beneath."
כְּנָפָיו	Nfp con (כָּנָף), "wing, skirt (of a garment)," + 3mps ps.

2:13

וַתֹּאמֶר אֶמְצָא־חֵן בְּעֵינֶיךָ אֲדֹנִי כִּי נִחַמְתָּנִי וְכִי דִבַּרְתָּ עַל־לֵב שִׁפְחָתֶךָ וְאָנֹכִי לֹא אֶהְיֶה כְּאַחַת שִׁפְחֹתֶיךָ:

אֶמְצָא־חֵן	See 2:2.
אֲדֹנִי	Nms con (אָדוֹן), "lord," + 1cs ps.
נִחַמְתָּנִי	Piel suff 2fs (נחם), "to comfort, console," + 1cs ps.
דִבַּרְתָּ	Piel suff 2ms (דָּבַר), "to speak."
לֵב	Nms, "heart, will, mind, inner person."
שִׁפְחָתֶךָ	Nfs con (שִׁפְחָה), "maid, maidservant," + 2ms ps.
וְאָנֹכִי	Conj (concessive), "although," + pron ip

Chapter 2

	(see 2:10), used for emphasis.
אֶהְיֶה	Qal pref 1cs (הָיָה; see 1:1).
כְּאַחַת	Prep + adj fs (אֶחָד), "one."

2:14

וַיֹּאמֶר לָה בֹעַז לְעֵת הָאֹכֶל גֹּשִׁי הֲלֹם וְאָכַלְתְּ מִן־הַלֶּחֶם וְטָבַלְתְּ פִּתֵּךְ בַּחֹמֶץ וַתֵּשֶׁב מִצַּד הַקּוֹצְרִים וַיִּצְבָּט־לָהּ קָלִי וַתֹּאכַל וַתִּשְׂבַּע וַתֹּתַר׃

לְעֵת	Prep (temporal use), "at," + nm/fs, "time."
הָאֹכֶל	Art + nms, "food"; לְעֵת + הָאֹכֶל = "at meal-time."
גֹּשִׁי	Qal impv fs (נָגַשׁ), "to draw near, approach."
הֲלֹם	Adv. "here."
וְאָכַלְתְּ	Qal suff w/c 2fs (אָכַל), "to eat."
מִן	See 1:1.
הַלֶּחֶם	Art + nms (see 1:6).
וְטָבַלְתְּ	Qal suff w/c 2fs (טָבַל), "to dip."
פִּתֵּךְ	Nfs con (פַּת), "fragment, bit, morsel of bread," + 2fs ps.
בַּחֹמֶץ	Prep + art + nms, "vinegar."
וַתֵּשֶׁב	See 1:4.
מִצַּד	Prep + nms (צַד), "side" = "at the side of."
הַקּוֹצְרִים	See 2:5.
וַיִּצְבָּט	Qal pret w/c 3ms (צָבַט), "to reach out, hold, grasp."

קָלִי	Nms, "parched grain."
וַתֹּאכַל	Qal pret w/c 3fs.
וַתִּשְׂבַּע	Qal pret w/c 3fs (שָׂבַע), "to be sated, satisfied."
וַתֹּתַר	Hiph pret w/c 3fs (יָתַר), "to leave, save, have more than enough."

2:15

וַתָּקָם לְלַקֵּט וַיְצַו בֹּעַז אֶת־נְעָרָיו לֵאמֹר גַּם בֵּין הָעֳמָרִים תְּלַקֵּט וְלֹא תַכְלִימוּהָ׃

וַתָּקָם	See 1:6. The conj, translated "when," initiates a dependent (temporal) clause.
לְלַקֵּט	Prep + Piel inf con (see 2:2).
וַיְצַו	Piel pret w/c 3ms (צָוָה; see 2:9). The conjunction initiates the main clause.
נְעָרָיו	Nmp con (נַעַר; see 2:5) + 3ms ps.
לֵאמֹר	Prep + Qal inf con (אָמַר; see 1:8).
גַּם	See 1:5.
בֵּין	Prep (see 1:17).
הָעֳמָרִים	Art + nmp (עֹמֶר; see 2:7).
תְּלַקֵּט	Piel pref 3fs (לָקַט; see 2:2), the prefixed reflecting injunction, "let."
תַכְלִימוּהָ	Hiph pref 2mp (כָּלַם), "to put to shame, humiliate, insult, rebuke," + 3fs ps.

2:16

וְגַם שֹׁל־תָּשֹׁלּוּ לָהּ מִן־הַצְּבָתִים וַעֲזַבְתֶּם וְלִקְּטָה וְלֹא תִגְעֲרוּ־בָהּ׃

Chapter 2

שֹׁל	Qal inf abs (שָׁלַל), here conveying the sense of command, e.g. "be sure" (cf. *IBHS*, §35.3.1g).
תָּשֹׁלּוּ	Qal pref 2mp (שָׁלַל), "to draw out."
הַצְּבָתִים	Art + nmp (צֶבֶת), "bundle."
וַעֲזַבְתֶּם	Qal suff w/c 2mp (עָזַב; see 1:16).
וְלִקְּטָה	Piel suff w/c 3fs (לָקַט; see 2:2). Conjunction denotes purpose ("so that").
תִגְעֲרוּ	Qal pref 2mp (גָּעַר), "to rebuke."
בָהּ	See 1:14. The preposition marks the object of the verb and may be left untranslated.

2:17

וַתְּלַקֵּט בַּשָּׂדֶה עַד־הָעָרֶב וַתַּחְבֹּט אֵת אֲשֶׁר־לִקֵּטָה וַיְהִי כְּאֵיפָה שְׂעֹרִים׃

וַתְּלַקֵּט	See 2:3. Logical use of the conjunction, "so."
הָעָרֶב	Art + nms (עֶרֶב), "evening."
וַתַּחְבֹּט	Qal pret w/c 3fs (חָבַט), "to beat off/out." Temporal use of the conjunction, "then."
לִקֵּטָה	Piel suff 3fs (לָקַט; see 2:2).
וַיְהִי	See 1:1.
כְּאֵיפָה	Prep + nfs, "ephah."
שְׂעֹרִים	See 1:22.

2:18

וַתִּשָּׂא֙ וַתָּב֣וֹא הָעִ֔יר וַתֵּ֥רֶא חֲמוֹתָ֖הּ אֵ֣ת אֲשֶׁר־לִקֵּ֑טָה וַתּוֹצֵ֣א וַתִּתֶּן־לָ֔הּ אֵ֥ת אֲשֶׁר־הוֹתִ֖רָה מִשָּׂבְעָֽהּ׃

וַתִּשָּׂא	Qal pret w/c 3fs (נָשָׂא), "to lift, carry."
וַתָּבוֹא	See 2:3.
הָעִיר	See 1:19.
וַתֵּרֶא	See 1:18.
חֲמוֹתָהּ	Nfs con (חָמוֹת; see 1:14) + 3fs ps.
וַתּוֹצֵא	Hiph pret w/c 3fs (יָצָא), "to bring out."
וַתִּתֶּן	Qal pret w/c 3fs (נָתַן; see 1:6), "to give."
הוֹתִרָה	Hiph suff 3fs (יָתַר; see 2:14).
מִשָּׂבְעָהּ	Prep (temporal use), "after," + nms con (שֹׂבַע), "satiety, abundance," + 3fs ps.

2:19

וַתֹּאמֶר֩ לָ֨הּ חֲמוֹתָ֜הּ אֵיפֹ֨ה לִקַּ֤טְתְּ הַיּוֹם֙ וְאָ֣נָה עָשִׂ֔ית יְהִ֥י מַכִּירֵ֖ךְ בָּר֑וּךְ וַתַּגֵּ֣ד לַחֲמוֹתָ֗הּ אֵ֤ת אֲשֶׁר־עָשְׂתָה֙ עִמּ֔וֹ וַתֹּ֗אמֶר שֵׁ֤ם הָאִישׁ֙ אֲשֶׁ֨ר עָשִׂ֧יתִי עִמּ֛וֹ הַיּ֖וֹם בֹּֽעַז׃

אֵיפֹה	Adv inter, "where?"
לִקַּטְתְּ	Piel suff 2fs (לָקַט; see 2:2).
הַיּוֹם	Art (functioning as demonstrative adj) + nms (יוֹם; see 1:1) = "today."
וְאָנָה	Conj + ptcl interrog (אָן), "where," + directional *hē'*.
עָשִׂית	See 2:11.
יְהִי	Qal juss 3ms (הָיָה; see 1:1).
מַכִּירֵךְ	Hiph act ptcp ms (נָכַר), "to regard,

Chapter 2

	recognize, acknowledge with honor, be acquainted with, distinguish," + 2fs ps.
בָּרוּךְ	Qal pass ptcp ms (בָּרַךְ), "to be blessed."
וַתַּגֵּד	Hiph pret w/c 3fs (נָגַד), "to declare."
לַחֲמוֹתָהּ	See 1:14.
עָשְׂתָה	Qal suff 3fs (עָשָׂה; see 1:8).
עִמּוֹ	See 1:6.
שֵׁם	See 1:2.
הָאִישׁ	See 1:2.
עָשִׂיתִי	Qal suff 1cs (עָשָׂה; see 1:8).
עִמּוֹ	See 1:6.

2:20

וַתֹּאמֶר נָעֳמִי לְכַלָּתָהּ בָּרוּךְ הוּא לַיהוָה אֲשֶׁר לֹא־עָזַב חַסְדּוֹ אֶת־הַחַיִּים וְאֶת־הַמֵּתִים וַתֹּאמֶר לָהּ נָעֳמִי קָרוֹב לָנוּ הָאִישׁ מִגֹּאֲלֵנוּ הוּא׃

לְכַלָּתָהּ	Prep + nfs con (כַּלָּה; see 1:6) + 3fs ps.
הוּא	Pron ip (see 1:1).
לַיהוָה	Prep + npr (see 1:6).
עָזַב	Qal suff 3ms (see 1:16).
חַסְדּוֹ	Nms con (חֶסֶד; see 1:8) + 3ms ps.
הַחַיִּים	Art + adj mp (חַי), "alive, living."
הַמֵּתִים	See 1:8.
קָרוֹב	Adj ms, "near."
לָנוּ	Prep + 1cp ps.
הָאִישׁ	See 1:2.
מִגֹּאֲלֵנוּ	Prep (partitive use), "one of," + Qal act

ptcp ms (גֹּאֵל), "to redeem, act as kinsman, do the part of next of kin," + 1cp ps.

2:21

וַתֹּאמֶר רוּת הַמּוֹאֲבִיָּה גַּם כִּי־אָמַר אֵלַי עִם־הַנְּעָרִים אֲשֶׁר־לִי תִּדְבָּקִין עַד אִם־כִּלּוּ אֵת כָּל־הַקָּצִיר אֲשֶׁר־לִי׃

הַמּוֹאֲבִיָּה	See 1:22.
גַּם	See 1:5, but with כִּי = "and also" s.v. גַּם, 11, *HALOT*).
אָמַר	Qal suff 3ms, "to say."
אֵלַי	Prep + 1cs ps.
הַנְּעָרִים	See 2:9.
תִּדְבָּקִין	Qal pref 2fs (דָּבַק; see 1:14) + paragogic *nûn*. Injunctive use of the prefixed verb, similar to the imperative.
אִם	Ptcl hyp (here used temporally, "until"; cf. *GBH*, §166p).
כִּלּוּ	Piel suff 3cp (כָּלָה), "to complete, bring to an end, finish."
הַקָּצִיר	Art + nms (קָצִיר; see 1:22).

2:22

וַתֹּאמֶר נָעֳמִי אֶל־רוּת כַּלָּתָהּ טוֹב בִּתִּי כִּי תֵצְאִי עִם־נַעֲרוֹתָיו וְלֹא יִפְגְּעוּ־בָךְ בְּשָׂדֶה אַחֵר׃

כַּלָּתָהּ	See 1:22.

Chapter 2

טוֹב	Adj ms, "good, pleasant, agreeable" (predicative use, i.e., "[is] good").
בֵּתִי	See 2:2.
תֵּצְאִי	Qal pref 2fs (יָצָא; see 1:7).
נַעֲרוֹתָיו	Nfp con (נַעֲרָה; see 2:5) + 3ms ps.
יִפְגְּעוּ	Qal pref 3mp (פָּגַע; see 1:16).
אַחֵר	Adj ms, "another, other."

2:23

וַתִּדְבַּ֞ק בְּנַעֲרוֹ֥ת בֹּ֙עַז֙ לְלַקֵּ֔ט עַד־כְּל֥וֹת קְצִיר־הַשְּׂעֹרִ֖ים וּקְצִ֣יר הַֽחִטִּ֑ים וַתֵּ֖שֶׁב אֶת־חֲמוֹתָֽהּ׃

וַתִּדְבַּק	Qal pret w/c 3fs (דָּבַק; see 1:14).
בְּנַעֲרוֹת	Prep + nfp con (נַעֲרָה; see 2:5).
לְלַקֵּט	See 2:15.
כְּלוֹת	Qal inf con (substantive use, כָּלָה; see 2:21).
קְצִיר	See 1:22.
הַשְּׂעֹרִים	Art + nfp (שְׂעֹרָה; see 1:22).
הַחִטִּים	Art + nfp (חִטָּה), "wheat."
וַתֵּשֶׁב	See 2:14.

CHAPTER 3

3:1
וַתֹּאמֶר לָהּ נָעֳמִי חֲמוֹתָהּ בִּתִּי הֲלֹא אֲבַקֶּשׁ־לָךְ מָנוֹחַ אֲשֶׁר יִיטַב־לָךְ:

הֲלֹא	Adv inter + ptcl neg (written defectively).
אֲבַקֶּשׁ	Piel pref 1cs (בָּקַשׁ), "to seek, find."
לָךְ	Prep + 2fs ps.
מָנוֹחַ	Nms, "resting-place, rest." "Rest" is used here in the sense of security.
יִיטַב	Qal pref 3ms (יָטַב), "to be good, well, glad, pleasing."

3:2
וְעַתָּה הֲלֹא בֹעַז מֹדַעְתָּנוּ אֲשֶׁר הָיִית אֶת־נַעֲרוֹתָיו הִנֵּה־הוּא זֹרֶה אֶת־גֹּרֶן הַשְּׂעֹרִים הַלָּיְלָה:

וְעַתָּה	Conj + adv "now."
מֹדַעְתָּנוּ	Nfs con (מֹדַעַת), "kindred, kinship," + 1cp ps.
הָיִית	Qal suff 2fs (הָיָה; see 1:1).
נַעֲרוֹתָיו	See 2:22.
הִנֵּה	See 1:15.
הוּא	See 1:1.
זֹרֶה	Qal act ptcp ms (זָרָה), "to scatter, fan,

	winnow."
גֹּרֶן	Nfs (גֹּרֶן), "threshing-floor." Adverbial accusative of location, "*at* the threshing-floor."
הַשְּׂעֹרִים	See 2:23.
הַלָּיְלָה	See 1:12.

3:3

וְרָחַצְתְּ וָסַכְתְּ וְשַׂמְתְּ [כ= שִׂמְלֹתֵךְ] עָלַיִךְ [כ= וְיָרַדְתִּי] הַגֹּרֶן אַל־תִּוָּדְעִי לָאִישׁ עַד כַּלֹּתוֹ לֶאֱכֹל וְלִשְׁתּוֹת׃

וְרָחַצְתְּ	Qal suff w/c 2fs (רָחַץ), "to wash, bathe." Logical use of the conjunction, "therefore, so."
וָסַכְתְּ	Qal suff w/c 2fs (סוּךְ, סִיךְ), "to pour, anoint."[2]
וְשַׂמְתְּ	Qal suff w/c 2fs (שִׂים, שׂוּם), "to put, place, set."
כ = שִׂמְלֹתֵךְ	Nfs con (שִׂמְלָה), "wrapper, mantle, garment, clothes," + 2fs ps. The Kethiv transliterates as *śimlōtēk*, with the Qere supplying the customary *yôḏ*.
ק = שִׂמְלֹתַיִךְ	Nfp con. Although the Kethiv could be interpreted as a collective singular (e.g., "clothing"), the Masoretes preferred a plural noun.

---

[2] The verbs רָחַץ and סוּךְ can have a reflexive force (see *GBH*, §41a).

Chapter 3

עָלַיִךְ	Prep + 2fs ps.
וְיָרַדְתִּי = כ	Conj + Qal suff w/c 1cs (יָרַד), "to go down, descend."
וְיָרַדְתְּ = ק	Qal suff w/c 2fs. The context is clear that the subject is second person rather than first person.
הַגֹּרֶן	Art + nfs (see 3:2). The noun is an adverbial accusative (location, or termination), so the preposition "to" can be supplied.
תִּוָּדְעִי	Niph pref 2fs (יָדַע), "to be known, be made known." Causative-reflexive use of the Niphal (see *IBHS*, §23.4h).
לָאִישׁ	See 1:12.
כַּלֹּתוֹ	Piel inf con (כָּלָה; see 2:21) + 3ms ps.
לֶאֱכֹל	Prep (signals object infinitive, leave untranslated) + Qal inf con (אָכַל; see 2:14).
וְלִשְׁתּוֹת	Conj + prep (signals object infinitive, leave untranslated) + Qal inf con (שָׁתָה; see 2:9).

3:4

וִיהִי בְשָׁכְבוֹ וְיָדַעַתְּ אֶת־הַמָּקוֹם אֲשֶׁר יִשְׁכַּב־שָׁם וּבָאת וְגִלִּית מַרְגְּלֹתָיו [כ = וְשָׁכָבְתִּי] וְהוּא יַגִּיד לָךְ אֵת אֲשֶׁר תַּעֲשִׂין׃

וִיהִי	Conj + Qal pref (juss) 3ms (הָיָה; see 1:1). The conjunction translates as

	"when," and initiates a dependent (temporal) clause.
בְּשָׁכְבוֹ	Prep + Qal inf con (שָׁכַב), "to lie down," + 3ms ps.
וְיָדַעַתְּ	Qal suff w/c 2fs (יָדַע; see 2:11). The conjunction, translates as "that," and begins a dependent (result) clause.
הַמָּקוֹם	See 1:7.
יִשְׁכַּב	Qal pref 3ms (שָׁכַב).
שָׁם	See 1:2 (left untranslated).
וּבָאת	Qal suff w/c 2fs (בּוֹא; see 1:2). The conjunction denotes sequence, "then."
וְגִלִּית	Piel suff w/c 2fs (גָּלָה), "to uncover (nakedness); disclose, discover, lay bare."
מַרְגְּלֹתָיו	Nfp con (מַרְגְּלוֹת*), "place of the feet, feet," + 3ms ps.
כ = וְשָׁכָבְתִּי	Qal suff w/c 1cs (שָׁכַב), unless the vocalization represents an archaic or anomalous 2fs.
ק = וְשָׁכָבְתְּ	Qal suff w/c 2fs (שָׁכַב). The Qere reflects the normal pointing of the 2fs suffix.
וְהוּא	Conj + pron ip 3ms. Emphatic, "himself."
יַגִּיד	Hiph pref 3ms (נָגַד; see 2:19).
לָךְ	See 3:1
תַּעֲשִׂין	Qal pref 2fs + paragogic *nûn* (עָשָׂה; see 1:8).

Chapter 3

3:5

וַתֹּאמֶר אֵלֶיהָ כֹּל אֲשֶׁר־תֹּאמְרִי [ק= אֵלַי] אֶעֱשֶׂה׃

וַתֹּאמֶר	See 1:8.
אֵלֶיהָ	See 1:18.
כֹּל	See 1:19.
תֹּאמְרִי	Qal pref 2fs (אָמַר).
ק= אֵלַי	Prep + 1cs ps. The Masoretes added this compound (hence there is no "כ=" siglum), but it is unnecessary since the meaning is clear without it.
אֶעֱשֶׂה	Qal pref 1cs (עָשָׂה; see 1:8).

3:6

וַתֵּרֶד הַגֹּרֶן וַתַּעַשׂ כְּכֹל אֲשֶׁר־צִוַּתָּה חֲמוֹתָהּ׃

וַתֵּרֶד	Qal pret w/c 3fs (יָרַד; see 3:3).
וַתַּעַשׂ	Qal pret w/c 3fs (עָשָׂה; see 1:8).
כְּכֹל	Prep + nms (כָּל; see 1:19).
צִוַּתָּה	Piel suff 3fs (צָוָה; see 2:9) + 3fs ps.

3:7

וַיֹּאכַל בֹּעַז וַיֵּשְׁתְּ וַיִּיטַב לִבּוֹ וַיָּבֹא לִשְׁכַּב בִּקְצֵה הָעֲרֵמָה וַתָּבֹא בַלָּט וַתְּגַל מַרְגְּלֹתָיו וַתִּשְׁכָּב׃

וַיֹּאכַל	Qal pret w/c 3ms (אָכַל; see 2:14). The conjunction translates as "when," and initiates a dependent (temporal) clause.
וַיֵּשְׁתְּ	Qal pret w/c 3ms (שָׁתָה; see 2:9).

וַיִּיטַב	Qal pret w/c 3ms (יָטַב; see 3:1).
לִבּוֹ	Nms con (לֵב; see 2:13) + 3ms ps.
וַיָּבֹא	Qal pret w/c 3ms (בּוֹא; see 1:2). The conjunction initiates the main clause and can be left untranslated.
לִשְׁכַּב	Prep + Qal inf con (שָׁכַב; see 3:4).
בִּקְצֵה	Prep + nms con (קָצֶה), "end, extremity."
הָעֲרֵמָה	Art + nfs, "heap."
וַתָּבֹא	Qal pret w/c 3fs (בּוֹא).
בַלָּט	Prep + art + nms, "secrecy, mystery."
וַתְּגַל	Piel pret w/c 3fs (גָּלָה; see 3:4).
וַתִּשְׁכָּב	Qal pret w/c 3fs (שָׁכַב; see 3:4).

3:8

וַיְהִי בַּחֲצִי הַלַּיְלָה וַיֶּחֱרַד הָאִישׁ וַיִּלָּפֵת וְהִנֵּה אִשָּׁה שֹׁכֶבֶת מַרְגְּלֹתָיו:

בַּחֲצִי	Prep + art + nms, "half."
וַיֶּחֱרַד	Qal pret w/c 3ms (חָרַד), "to tremble, be terrified, start, be startled."
הָאִישׁ	See 1:2.
וַיִּלָּפֵת	Niph pret w/c 3ms (לָפַת), "to turn, turn aside, be twisted."
וְהִנֵּה	See 2:4.
שֹׁכֶבֶת	Qal act ptcp fs (שָׁכַב; see 3:4).

3:9

וַיֹּאמֶר מִי־אָתְּ וַתֹּאמֶר אָנֹכִי רוּת אֲמָתֶךָ וּפָרַשְׂתָּ

Chapter 3

כְּנָפֶ֙ךָ֙ עַל־אֲמָ֣תְךָ֔ כִּ֥י גֹאֵ֖ל אָֽתָּה׃

מִי	Pron inter.
אַתְּ	Pron ip 2fs.
אָנֹכִי	Pron ip 1cs.
אֲמָתֶךָ	Nfs con (אָמָה), "maid, maidservant," + 2ms ps.
וּפָרַשְׂתָּ	Qal suff w/c 2ms (פָּרַשׂ), "to spread, spread out." Logical use of the conjunction, "so."
כְּנָפֶךָ	Nfs con (כָּנָף; see 2:12) + 2ms ps.
גֹאֵל	Qal act ptcp ms (גָּאַל; see 2:20), used nominally, i.e., "redeemer," in the sense of a close relative, or next-of-kin.
אָתָּה	Pron ip 2ms.

3:10

וַיֹּ֗אמֶר בְּרוּכָ֨ה אַ֤תְּ לַֽיהוָה֙ בִּתִּ֔י הֵיטַ֛בְתְּ חַסְדֵּ֥ךְ הָאַחֲר֖וֹן מִן־הָרִאשׁ֑וֹן לְבִלְתִּי־לֶ֗כֶת אַחֲרֵי֙ הַבַּ֣חוּרִ֔ים אִם־דַּ֖ל וְאִם־עָשִֽׁיר׃

בְּרוּכָה	Qal pass ptcp fs (בָּרַךְ; see 2:19).
אַתְּ	Pron ip 2fs.
לַיהוָה	See 2:20.
הֵיטַבְתְּ	Hiph suff 2fs (יָטַב), "to make glad, rejoice; to do good to, deal well with."
חַסְדֵּךְ	Nms con (חֶסֶד; see 1:8) + 2fs ps.
הָאַחֲרוֹן	Art, functioning as pron dem, "this" (*IBHS*, §13.5.2) + adj ms, "coming after,

	behind; latter, last."
מִן	Prep (comparative; see 1:13).
הָרִאשׁוֹן	Art + adj ms, "first."
לְבִלְתִּי	See 1:13.
לֶכֶת	Qal inf con (הָלַךְ; see 1:1).
אַחֲרֵי	See 1:15.
הַבַּחוּרִים	Art + nmp (בָּחוּר), "young man."
אִם	Adv, "whether."
דַּל	Adj ms con, "low, weak, poor, thin."
וְאִם	Conj (alternative), "or," + adv, "whether" (second occurrence may be left untranslated).
עָשִׁיר	Adj ms, "rich."

3:11

וְעַתָּה בִּתִּי אַל־תִּירְאִי כֹּל אֲשֶׁר־תֹּאמְרִי אֶעֱשֶׂה־לָּךְ כִּי יוֹדֵעַ כָּל־שַׁעַר עַמִּי כִּי אֵשֶׁת חַיִל אָתְּ:

וְעַתָּה	See 3:2.
תִּירְאִי	Qal pref 2fs (יָרֵא), "to fear."
תֹּאמְרִי	See 3:5.
אֶעֱשֶׂה	See 3:5.
יוֹדֵעַ	Qal act ptcp ms (יָדַע; see 2:11).
שַׁעַר	Nms con, "gate."
עַמִּי	Nms con (עַם; see 1:6) + 1cs ps.
אֵשֶׁת	Nfs con (אִשָּׁה; see 1:1).
חַיִל	See 2:1; here, "worth."[3]

---

[3] On the noun as conveying the idea of worth, cf. Robin

CHAPTER 3

3:12

וְעַתָּה֙ כִּ֣י אָמְנָ֔ם כִּ֥י [כ= אִם] גֹּאֵ֖ל אָנֹ֑כִי וְגַ֛ם יֵ֥שׁ גֹּאֵ֖ל קָר֥וֹב מִמֶּֽנִּי׃

כִּי	Conjunction, used asseveratively, "truly" (cf. *GBH*, §164b).
אָמְנָם	Adv, "verily, truly."
כ= אִם	Ptcl hyp (untranslated). כִּי אָמְנָם כִּי is itself problematic because the second כִּי is superfluous. Read with the Qere, which omits אִם (probably a dittography).[4]
גֹּאֵל	See 3:9.
אָנֹכִי	See 3:9.
וְגַם	See 1:12.
יֵשׁ	See 1:12.
קָרוֹב	See 2:20.
מִמֶּנִּי	Prep (comparative) + 1cs ps.

3:13

לִ֣ינִי הַלַּ֗יְלָה וְהָיָ֤ה בַבֹּ֙קֶר֙ אִם־יִגְאָלֵ֥ךְ טוֹב֙ יִגְאָ֔ל וְאִם־לֹ֨א יַחְפֹּ֧ץ לְגָֽאֳלֵ֛ךְ וּגְאַלְתִּ֥יךְ אָנֹ֖כִי חַי־יְהוָ֑ה שִׁכְבִ֖י עַד־הַבֹּֽקֶר׃

Wakely, "חַיִל," in *New International Dictionary of Old Testament Theology and Exegesis* (Willem A. VanGemeren, ed.; Grand Rapids, MI: Zondervan, 1997), 2: 116-18.

[4] See Daniel I. Block, *Judges, Ruth* (NAC; Nashville: Broadman & Holman, 1999), 695, n. 49.

לִינִי	Qal impv fs (לוּן/לִין; see 1:16).
הַלַּיְלָה	See 1:12. "Tonight" is an equivalent.
וְהָיָה	Qal suff w/c 3ms (see 1:1).
בַבֹּקֶר	Prep + art + nms (בֹּקֶר; see 2:7).
אִם	Ptcl hyp, "if."
יִגְאַל	Qal pref 3ms (juss; see 2:20).
יַחְפֹּץ	Qal pref 3ms (חָפֵץ), "to delight in."
לְגָאֳלֵךְ	Prep + Qal inf con (גָּאַל) + 2fs ps.
וּגְאַלְתִּיךְ	Qal suff w/c 1cs (גָּאַל) + 2fs.
אָנֹכִי	Pron ip 1cs. Since the preceding verb, וּגְאַלְתִּיךְ, supplies the subject of the verb (first person), the pronoun is emphatic, "myself."
חַי	Adj ms (see 2:20). Used in the oath formula "as Yahweh lives."
יְהוָה	See 1:6.
שִׁכְבִי	Qal impv fs (see 3:4).
הַבֹּקֶר	See 2:7.

3:14

וַתִּשְׁכַּב [כ= מַרְגְּלֹתָו] עַד־הַבֹּקֶר וַתָּקָם [כ= בְּטֶרוֹם] יַכִּיר אִישׁ אֶת־רֵעֵהוּ וַיֹּאמֶר אַל־יִוָּדַע כִּי־בָאָה הָאִשָּׁה הַגֹּרֶן:

וַתִּשְׁכַּב	See 3:7.
כ= מַרְגְּלֹתָו	Nfp con (see 3:4) + 3ms ps, "place of his feet." The *yôḏ* helping vowel of the 3ms ps has dropped out.
ק= מַרְגְּלוֹתָיו	Nfp con (see 3:4) + 3ms ps, "place of his

CHAPTER 3

	feet."
וַתָּקָם	See 1:6.
כ= בִּטְרוֹם	Prep + prep, "before." This is an alternate form of the usual (Qere) form.
ק= בְּטֶרֶם	Prep + prep, "before."
יַכִּיר	Hiph pref 3ms (נָכַר; see 2:10).
אִישׁ	See 1:1. The noun can be used to express a general third person, e.g., "one," "someone." With רֵעַ it expresses reciprocity, e.g., "one another," "each other" (see *GBH,* §147b, c).
רֵעֵהוּ	Nms con (רֵיעַ/רֵעַ), "friend, companion, fellow, another person," + 3ms ps.
יִוָּדַע	Niph pref (juss) 3ms (יָדַע; see 3:3).
בָאָה	Qal suff 3fs (בּוֹא; see 1:2).
הָאִשָּׁה	See 1:5.
הַגֹּרֶן	See 3:3.

3:15

וַיֹּאמֶר הָבִי הַמִּטְפַּחַת אֲשֶׁר־עָלַיִךְ וְאֶחֳזִי־בָהּ וַתֹּאחֶז בָּהּ וַיָּמָד שֵׁשׁ־שְׂעֹרִים וַיָּשֶׁת עָלֶיהָ וַיָּבֹא הָעִיר׃

הָבִי	Qal impv fs (יָהַב), "to give."
הַמִּטְפַּחַת	Art + nfs, "cloak."
עָלַיִךְ	Prep + 2fs ps.
וְאֶחֳזִי	Conj + Qal impv fs (אָחַז), "to grasp, take hold of."
בָהּ	Prep (object of verb of touching),

	"onto," + 3fs ps.
וַתֹּאחֶז	Qal pret w/c 3fs (אָחַז).
וַיָּמָד	Qal pret 3ms (מָדַד; a geminate verb, see מַר, 1:13), "to measure."
שֵׁשׁ	Adj fs, "six."
שְׂעֹרִים	See 1:22.
וַיָּשֶׁת	Qal pret w/c 3ms (שִׁית), "to put, set."
עָלֶיהָ	Prep (accompaniment), "with," + 3fs ps.
וַיָּבֹא	See 3:7.
הָעִיר	See 1:19.

3:16

וַתָּבוֹא אֶל־חֲמוֹתָהּ וַתֹּאמֶר מִי־אַתְּ בִּתִּי וַתַּגֶּד־לָהּ אֵת כָּל־אֲשֶׁר עָשָׂה־לָהּ הָאִישׁ:

וַתָּבוֹא	See 2:3.
חֲמוֹתָהּ	See 2:18.
מִי־אַתְּ	Pron inter, "who," + pron ip 2fs. This noun clause translates lit., "who are you?" but Naomi would certainly have known Ruth. Block remarks on the flexibility with which interrogatives are used, and classifies this one as "an accusative of condition, that is, 'In what condition or state are you?'" or, "how are you?"[5]
וַתַּגֶּד	See 2:19.

---

[5] Block, *Judges, Ruth*, 699.

Chapter 3

עָשָׂה	Qal suff 3ms (see 1:8).

3:17

וַתֹּאמֶר שֵׁשׁ־הַשְּׂעֹרִים הָאֵלֶּה נָתַן לִי כִּי אָמַר [ק=
אֵלַי] אַל־תָּבוֹאִי רֵיקָם אֶל־חֲמוֹתֵךְ:

הַשְּׂעֹרִים	See 2:23.
הָאֵלֶּה	Art + adj cp, "these."
נָתַן	Qal suff 3ms (see 1:6).
אָמַר	See 2:21.
ק= אֵלַי	Prep + 1cs ps. The Kethiv lacks אֵלַי, which the Qere adds; but as in 3:5, the Kethiv is sufficient.
תָּבוֹאִי	Qal pref (jussive) 2fs (בּוֹא; see 1:2).
רֵיקָם	Adv. "emptily, vainly."
חֲמוֹתֵךְ	See 2:11.

3:18

וַתֹּאמֶר שְׁבִי בִתִּי עַד אֲשֶׁר תֵּדְעִין אֵיךְ יִפֹּל דָּבָר כִּי
לֹא יִשְׁקֹט הָאִישׁ כִּי־אִם־כִּלָּה הַדָּבָר הַיּוֹם:

שְׁבִי	Qal impv fs (יָשַׁב; see 1:4).
עַד אֲשֶׁר	Prep + pron rel. Lit. "until when," but אֲשֶׁר can be omitted from the translation.
תֵּדְעִין	Qal pref 2fs (יָדַע; see 2:11) + paragogic *nûn*.
אֵיךְ	Adv inter, "how?"
יִפֹּל	Qal pref 3ms (נָפַל; see 2:10), used here

	in the sense of "turn out," "be resolved."
דָּבָר	Nms, "word, thing, matter."
יִשְׁקֹט	Qal pref 3ms (שָׁקַט), "to be quiet, be at rest, undisturbed, inactive."
כִּי־אִם	Conj + ptcl hyp, lit., "except if" (cf. s.v. II כִּי, 4, *HALOT*), but translated "unless."
כִּלָּה	Piel suff 3ms (כָּלָה; see 2:21).
הַדָּבָר	Art + nms.
הַיּוֹם	See 2:19.

CHAPTER 4

4:1

וּבֹעַז עָלָה הַשַּׁעַר וַיֵּשֶׁב שָׁם וְהִנֵּה הַגֹּאֵל עֹבֵר אֲשֶׁר דִּבֶּר־בֹּעַז וַיֹּאמֶר סוּרָה שְׁבָה־פֹּה פְּלֹנִי אַלְמֹנִי וַיָּסַר וַיֵּשֵׁב׃

עָלָה	Qal suff 3ms, "to go up, ascend, climb."
הַשַּׁעַר	Art + nms (see 3:11).[6]
וַיֵּשֶׁב	Qal pret w/c 3ms (יָשַׁב; see 1:4).
שָׁם	See 1:2.
וְהִנֵּה	See 2:4.
הַגֹּאֵל	Art + Qal act ptcp ms (see 2:20).
עֹבֵר	Qal act ptcp ms (see 2:8).
דִּבֶּר	See 3:18.
סוּרָה	Qal impv ms (סוּר), "to turn aside," + paragogic *hē*.
שְׁבָה	Qal impv ms (יָשַׁב; see 1:4) + paragogic *hē*.
פֹּה	Adv, "here."
פְּלֹנִי	Adj ms, "a certain one," and always appearing with אַלְמֹנִי.
אַלְמֹנִי	Adj ms, "someone, a certain [name unspoken], + אַלְמֹנִי = "friend."

---

[6] The city gate was the place where official business and decisions were taken by the elders.

וַיָּסַר	Qal pret w/c 3ms (סוּר).

4:2

וַיִּקַּח עֲשָׂרָה אֲנָשִׁים מִזִּקְנֵי הָעִיר וַיֹּאמֶר שְׁבוּ־פֹה וַיֵּשֵׁבוּ:

וַיִּקַּח	Qal pret w/c 3ms (לָקַח), "to take."
עֲשָׂרָה	Adj fs (עֶשֶׂר), "ten."
אֲנָשִׁים	Nmp (אִישׁ; see 1:1).[7]
מִזִּקְנֵי	Prep + adj mp con (זָקֵן), "old."
הָעִיר	See 1:19.
שְׁבוּ	Qal impv mp (יָשַׁב; see 1:4).
וַיֵּשֵׁבוּ	See 1:4.

4:3

וַיֹּאמֶר לַגֹּאֵל חֶלְקַת הַשָּׂדֶה אֲשֶׁר לְאָחִינוּ לֶאֱלִימֶלֶךְ מָכְרָה נָעֳמִי הַשָּׁבָה מִשְּׂדֵה מוֹאָב:

חֶלְקַת	See 2:3.
לְאָחִינוּ	Prep + nms con (אָח), "brother," + 1cp ps.
לֶאֱלִימֶלֶךְ	Prep + npr (see 1:2). The preposition denotes apposition to אָחִינוּ and as such is untranslated.
מָכְרָה	Qal suff 3fs (מָכַר), "to sell." Perfect of

---

[7] The custom was for at least two witnesses to be present for a transaction or decision to be valid (cf. Deut 17:6; 19:15; 30:19).

Chapter 4

	resolve (*IBHS,* §30.5.1d), translated in present time.
הַשֵּׁבָה	See 1:22.
מִשְּׂדֵה	Prep + nms con (see 2:6).

4:4

וַאֲנִ֨י אָמַ֜רְתִּי אֶגְלֶ֧ה אָזְנְךָ֣ לֵאמֹ֗ר קְ֠נֵה נֶ֥גֶד הַיֹּשְׁבִים֮
וְנֶ֣גֶד זִקְנֵ֣י עַמִּי֒ אִם־תִּגְאַל֙ גְּאָ֔ל וְאִם־לֹ֨א יִגְאַ֜ל הַגִּ֣ידָה
לִּ֗י [כ= וְאֵדְעָ֔] כִּ֣י אֵ֤ין זוּלָֽתְךָ֙ לִגְא֔וֹל וְאָנֹכִ֖י אַחֲרֶ֑יךָ
וַיֹּ֖אמֶר אָנֹכִ֥י אֶגְאָֽל׃

וַאֲנִי	Conj + pron ip 1cs.
אָמַרְתִּי	See 1:12. The verb can also mean "I said to myself," or, "I thought."
אֶגְלֶה	Qal pref 1cs (גָּלָה), "to uncover."
אָזְנְךָ	Nfs con (אֹזֶן), "ear," + 2ms ps, + אֶגְלֶה = lit. "I would uncover your ear," but idiomatic for, "to reveal, disclose."
לֵאמֹר	See 2:15.
קְנֵה	Qal impv ms (קָנָה), "to get, acquire."
נֶגֶד	Prep, "in front (of), in sight (of), opposite to."
הַיֹּשְׁבִים	Art + Qal act ptcp mp (יָשַׁב).
זִקְנֵי	Adj mp con (see 4:2).
עַמִּי	See 1:16.
אִם	Ptcl hyp, "if" (both times in the verse).
תִּגְאַל	Qal pref 2ms (גָּאַל; see 2:20).
גְּאָל	Qal impv ms.
יִגְאַל	See 3:13. A number of Hebrew

59

manuscripts and a number of versions (e.g., the Septuagint) read 2ms here, i.e., "you will redeem." The Masoretic text, "but if he will not redeem it," is the more difficult reading, which generally is to be preferred. However, here it has probably corrupted from an original 2ms, so read with the variants.[8] Otherwise we must envision Boaz first addressing the redeemer ("if you will redeem it, redeem it"), then turning to address the elders ("but if he will not redeem it"), and then turning back to the redeemer ("tell me . . .").

הַגִּידָה   Hiph impv ms (נָגַד) + paragogic *hē'*, "to declare, tell."

כ = וְאֵדַע   Conj + Qal pref (coh in meaning but not form) 1cs (יָדַע; see 2:11). It is not inconceivable that the Kethiv preserves a different vocalization, but the likelihood is that the final *hē'* has dropped out.

ק = וְאֵדְעָה   Conj (purpose), "so that," + Qal coh 1cs.
אֵין   Ptcl neg.
זוּלָתְךָ   Prep, "except, besides," + 2ms ps.

---

[8] If the following imperative (הַגִּידָה) were plural, then the Masoretic text could perhaps be understood as Boaz addressing the elders, "If he will he will not redeem, you [elders] declare [it] to me…"

Chapter 4

לִגְאוֹל	Prep + Qal inf con.
וְאָנֹכִי	See 2:10. The pronoun is emphatic, but apply the emphasis to the verb.
אַחֲרֶיךָ	Adv (see 1:15) + 2ms ps.
אֶגְאָל	Qal pref 1cs.

4:5

וַיֹּאמֶר בֹּעַז בְּיוֹם־קְנוֹתְךָ הַשָּׂדֶה מִיַּד נָעֳמִי וּמֵאֵת רוּת הַמּוֹאֲבִיָּה אֵשֶׁת־הַמֵּת [כ= קָנִיתִי] לְהָקִים שֵׁם־הַמֵּת עַל־נַחֲלָתוֹ׃

בְּיוֹם	Prep + nms (יוֹם; see 1:1).
קְנוֹתְךָ	Qal inf con (קָנָה; see 4:4) + 2ms ps.
מִיַּד	Prep + nfs con (יָד; see 1:13).
וּמֵאֵת	Conj (adjunctive), "also," + prep + prep = lit. "from proximity with," but render only the conjunction into the translation.
הַמּוֹאֲבִיָּה	See 1:22.
אֵשֶׁת	See 3:11.
הַמֵּת	Art + Qal act ptcp ms (מוּת; see 1:3).
כ= קָנִיתִי	Qal suff 1cs (קָנָה). The Kethiv is probably a corruption from the 1cs, since the context makes it clear that the verb must be second person.
ק= קָנִיתָה	Qal suff 2ms (קָנָה) + 3fs ps.
לְהָקִים	Prep + Hiph inf con (קוּם), "to raise."
הַמֵּת	Art + Qal act ptcp ms (מוּת; see 1:8).
עַל	Prep (advantage), "for the sake of, on

	behalf of."
נַחֲלָתוֹ	Nfs con (נַחֲלָה), "inheritance, right of redemption," + 3ms ps.

4:6

וַיֹּאמֶר הַגֹּאֵל לֹא אוּכַל [כ= לִגְאוֹל]־לִי פֶּן־אַשְׁחִית
אֶת־נַחֲלָתִי גְּאַל־לְךָ אַתָּה אֶת־גְּאֻלָּתִי כִּי לֹא־אוּכַל
לִגְאֹל:

אוּכַל	Qal pref 1cs (יָכֹל), "to be able." This is a I-ו verb (i.e., וכל), which has *šûreq* for the prefix vowel instead of the usual *segôl* for the 1cs.
כ = לִגְאוֹל	Prep + Qal inf con (גָּאַל). The Masoretic text is either a corruption or an alternative form. The Qere is the standard form.
ק = לִגְאֹל	Prep + Qal inf con.
פֶּן	Conj, "lest."
אַשְׁחִית	Hiph pref 1cs (שָׁחַת), "to spoil, ruin." The Hiphil here expresses an ingressive aspect (*GBH*, §54d).
נַחֲלָתִי	Nfs con (נַחֲלָה; see 4:5) + 1cs ps.
אַתָּה	See 3:9.
גְּאֻלָּתִי	Nfs con (גָּאַל) + 1cs ps.

4:7

וְזֹאת לְפָנִים בְּיִשְׂרָאֵל עַל־הַגְּאוּלָּה וְעַל־הַתְּמוּרָה
לְקַיֵּם כָּל־דָּבָר שָׁלַף אִישׁ נַעֲלוֹ וְנָתַן לְרֵעֵהוּ וְזֹאת

Chapter 4

הַתְּעוּדָה בְּיִשְׂרָאֵל:

וְזֹאת	Conj + pron dem fs, "this." Subject of noun clause (as is the second occurrence of the pronoun in the verse).
לְפָנִים	Prep + nmp (פָּנֶה; see 2:10); with the prep = "formerly."
בְּיִשְׂרָאֵל	Prep + nprg.
הַגְּאוּלָה	Art + nfs (see 4:6).
הַתְּמוּרָה	Art + nfs, "exchange, recompense."
לְקַיֵּם	Prep + Piel inf con (קוּם), "to fulfill, confirm, ratify."
דָּבָר	See 3:18.
שָׁלַף	Qal suff 3ms, "to draw out, off."
נַעֲלוֹ	Nfs con (נַעַל), "sandal," + 3ms ps.
וְנָתַן	Conj + Qal suff 3ms (see 1:6).
לְרֵעֵהוּ	Prep + nms con (רֵעַ; see 3:14) + 3ms ps.
הַתְּעוּדָה	Art + nfs, "testimony, attestation."

4:8

וַיֹּאמֶר הַגֹּאֵל לְבֹעַז קְנֵה־לָךְ וַיִּשְׁלֹף נַעֲלוֹ:

קְנֵה	See 4:4.
וַיִּשְׁלֹף	Qal pret w/c 3ms (see 4:7).

4:9

וַיֹּאמֶר בֹּעַז לַזְּקֵנִים וְכָל־הָעָם עֵדִים אַתֶּם הַיּוֹם כִּי קָנִיתִי אֶת־כָּל־אֲשֶׁר לֶאֱלִימֶלֶךְ וְאֵת כָּל־אֲשֶׁר לְכִלְיוֹן וּמַחְלוֹן מִיַּד נָעֳמִי:

לַזְּקֵנִים	Prep + art + adj mp (זָקֵן; see 4:2).
עֵדִים	Nmp (עֵד), "witness."
אַתֶּם	Pron ip 2mp.
לֶאֱלִימֶלֶךְ	See 4:3.
לְכִלְיוֹן	Prep + npr (see 1:2).
וּמַחְלוֹן	Conj + npr (see 1:2).
מִיַּד	See 4:5.

4:10

וְגַם אֶת־רוּת הַמֹּאֲבִיָּה אֵשֶׁת מַחְלוֹן קָנִיתִי לִי לְאִשָּׁה לְהָקִים שֵׁם־הַמֵּת עַל־נַחֲלָתוֹ וְלֹא־יִכָּרֵת שֵׁם־הַמֵּת מֵעִם אֶחָיו וּמִשַּׁעַר מְקוֹמוֹ עֵדִים אַתֶּם הַיּוֹם:

וְגַם	See 1:12.
קָנִיתִי	See קָנָה, 4:5.
לְהָקִים	See 4:5.
הַמֵּת	See 4:5.
נַחֲלָתוֹ	See 4:5.
יִכָּרֵת	Niph pref 3ms (כָּרַת), "to be cut off."
מֵעִם	Prep, "from," + prep, "with," the latter left untranslated.
אֶחָיו	Nmp con (אָח; see 4:3) + 3ms ps.
וּמִשַּׁעַר	Conj + prep + nms (שַׁעַר; see 3:11).
מְקוֹמוֹ	Nms con (מָקוֹם; see 1:7) + 3ms ps.

4:11

וַיֹּאמְרוּ כָּל־הָעָם אֲשֶׁר־בַּשַּׁעַר וְהַזְּקֵנִים עֵדִים יִתֵּן יְהוָה אֶת־הָאִשָּׁה הַבָּאָה אֶל־בֵּיתֶךָ כְּרָחֵל וּכְלֵאָה אֲשֶׁר בָּנוּ שְׁתֵּיהֶם אֶת־בֵּית יִשְׂרָאֵל וַעֲשֵׂה־חַיִל

Chapter 4

בְּאֶפְרָתָה וּקְרָא־שֵׁם בְּבֵית לָחֶם:

וַיֹּאמְרוּ	See 2:4.
בַּשַּׁעַר	Prep + art + nms (see 3:11).
וְהַזְּקֵנִים	Conj + art + adj mp (see 4:2).
יִתֵּן	See 1:9. Here, "make" (s.v. נָתַן, 2b, BDB), and expressing the jussive.
הָאִשָּׁה	See 1:5.
הַבָּאָה	Art + Qal act ptcp fs (בוֹא; see 1:2).
בֵּיתֶךָ	Nms con (בַּיִת; see 1:8) + 2ms ps.
כְּרָחֵל	Prep + npr, "Rachel."
וּכְלֵאָה	Conj + prep + npr, "Leah."
בָּנוּ	Qal suff 3cp (בָּנָה), "to build."
שְׁתֵּיהֶם	See 1:19.
בֵּית	See 1:9.
וַעֲשֵׂה	Conj + Qal impv ms (עָשָׂה), usually "to do, make," but here "to acquire" (s.v. I עשׂה, 6, *HALOT*). The imperative is somewhat unusual, as one would expect another jussive (the same applies to קְרָא). Such a sequence of jussive followed by imperative occurs after a jussive of permission (*GBH,* §114n), and it may be likewise for jussives of blessing as occurs here.
חַיִל	See 2:1.
בְּאֶפְרָתָה	Prep + npr, "Ephrathah."
וּקְרָא	Conj + Qal impv ms (קָרָא; see 1:20). קְרָא־שֵׁם, lit., "call a name," but

figuratively, "to give someone a name" (s.v. I קרא, A.2.a, *HALOT*), in the sense of fame. An alternative is "to restore a name," as in continuing the name of Mahlon.

בְּבֵית לָחֶם   See 1:19.

4:12

וִיהִ֤י בֵֽיתְךָ֙ כְּבֵ֣ית פֶּ֔רֶץ אֲשֶׁר־יָלְדָ֥ה תָמָ֖ר לִֽיהוּדָ֑ה מִן־הַזֶּ֗רַע אֲשֶׁ֨ר יִתֵּ֤ן יְהוָה֙ לְךָ֔ מִן־הַֽנַּעֲרָ֖ה הַזֹּֽאת׃

וִיהִי	Conj + Qal juss 3ms (הָיָה; see 1:1).
כְּבֵית	Prep + nms con.
פֶּרֶץ	Npr, "Perez."
יָלְדָה	Qal suff 3fs (יָלַד; see 1:12).
תָמָר	Npr, "Tamar."
לִיהוּדָה	Prep + npr.
הַזֶּרַע	Art + nms, "seed, offspring."
מִן	Prep (agency), "by."
הַנַּעֲרָה	See 2:5.
הַזֹּאת	See 2:5.

4:13

וַיִּקַּ֨ח בֹּ֤עַז אֶת־רוּת֙ וַתְּהִי־ל֣וֹ לְאִשָּׁ֔ה וַיָּבֹ֖א אֵלֶ֑יהָ וַיִּתֵּ֨ן יְהוָ֥ה לָ֛הּ הֵרָי֖וֹן וַתֵּ֥לֶד בֵּֽן׃

וַיִּקַּח	See 4:2.
וַתְּהִי	See 2:12.
וַיָּבֹא	See 3:7.

CHAPTER 4

אֵלֶיהָ	See 1:18.
וַיִּתֵּן	Qal pret w/c 3ms (נָתַן).
הֵרָיוֹן	Nms, "conception, pregnancy."
וַתֵּלֶד	Qal pret w/c 3fs (יָלַד).
בֵּן	Nms, "son."

4:14

וַתֹּאמַרְנָה הַנָּשִׁים אֶל־נָעֳמִי בָּרוּךְ יְהוָה אֲשֶׁר לֹא
הִשְׁבִּית לָךְ גֹּאֵל הַיּוֹם וְיִקָּרֵא שְׁמוֹ בְּיִשְׂרָאֵל:

וַתֹּאמַרְנָה	See 1:10.
הַנָּשִׁים	Art + nfp (אִשָּׁה; see 1:1).
בָּרוּךְ	See 2:19.
הִשְׁבִּית	Hiph suff 3ms (שָׁבַת), "to cause to cease, put an end to, destroy, remove, cause to fail, let be lacking.
וְיִקָּרֵא	Conj + Niph pref 3ms (קָרָא), "to be called, proclaimed."
שְׁמוֹ	Nms con (שֵׁם; see 1:2) + 3ms ps.

4:15

וְהָיָה לָךְ לְמֵשִׁיב נֶפֶשׁ וּלְכַלְכֵּל אֶת־שֵׂיבָתֵךְ כִּי
כַלָּתֵךְ אֲשֶׁר־אֲהֵבַתֶךְ יְלָדַתּוּ אֲשֶׁר־הִיא טוֹבָה לָךְ
מִשִּׁבְעָה בָּנִים:

וְהָיָה	See 3:13.
לְמֵשִׁיב	Prep + Hiph act ptcp ms (שׁוּב; see 1:21).
נֶפֶשׁ	Nfs, "soul, life, living being."
וּלְכַלְכֵּל	Conj + prep + Pilpel inf con (used

	nominally; (כּוּל), "to sustain, maintain, support, nourish."
שִׂיבָתֶךְ	Nfs con (שֵׂיבָה), "grey hair, old age."
כַּלָּתֵךְ	Nfs con (כַּלָּה; see 1:6).
אֲהֵבַתֶךְ	Qal suff 3fs (אָהֵב), "to love," + 2fs ps.
יְלָדַתּוּ	Qal suff 3fs (יָלַד) + 3ms ps.
הִיא	Pron ip 3fs, functioning predicatively in a noun clause (see *IBHS*, §8.4, 16.3.3), "is." On the association with אֲשֶׁר, see *GBH*, §158g.
טוֹבָה	Adj fs (טוֹב; see 2:22).
מִשִּׁבְעָה	Prep (comparative) + adj ms (שֶׁבַע), "seven."
בָּנִים	See 1:11.

4:16

וַתִּקַּח נָעֳמִי אֶת־הַיֶּלֶד וַתְּשִׁתֵהוּ בְחֵיקָהּ וַתְּהִי־לוֹ לְאֹמֶנֶת׃

וַתִּקַּח	Qal pret w/c 3fs (לָקַח; see 4:2).
הַיֶּלֶד	Art + nms (יֶלֶד; see 1:5).
וַתְּשִׁתֵהוּ	Qal pret w/c 3fs (שִׁית; see 3:15) + 3ms ps.
בְחֵיקָהּ	Prep (spatial), "at," + nms con (חֵיק), "bosom," + 3fs ps. Since Naomi was past the age of child-bearing (cf. 1:11-12), the idea here is "lap."
וַתְּהִי	Qal pret w/c 3fs (הָיָה; see 1:1).
לְאֹמֶנֶת	Prep + Qal act ptcp fs (אָמַן), "to

confirm, support; foster-father/mother, nurse." Nurse, in this verse, is used in the sense of attendant.

4:17

וַתִּקְרֶאנָה לוֹ הַשְּׁכֵנוֹת שֵׁם לֵאמֹר יֻלַּד־בֵּן לְנָעֳמִי וַתִּקְרֶאנָה שְׁמוֹ עוֹבֵד הוּא אֲבִי־יִשַׁי אֲבִי דָוִד:

וַתִּקְרֶאנָה	Qal pret w/c 3fp (קָרָא; see 1:20).
הַשְּׁכֵנוֹת	Art + nfp (שְׁכֵנָה), "inhabitant, neighbor."
יֻלַּד	Qal pass ptcp 3ms (יָלַד), "to be born."
לְנָעֳמִי	Prep + npr.
עוֹבֵד	Npr, "Obed."
הוּא	See 1:1.
אֲבִי	Nms con (see 2:11) + 1cs ps.
יִשַׁי	Npr, "Jesse."
דָוִד	Npr, "David."

4:18

וְאֵלֶּה תּוֹלְדוֹת פָּרֶץ פֶּרֶץ הוֹלִיד אֶת־חֶצְרוֹן:

וְאֵלֶּה	Conj + pron dem common plural.
תּוֹלְדוֹת	Nfp con (the absolute form does not occur in the Hebrew Bible, and is thus reconstructed as תּוֹלָדוֹת; see s.v. תּוֹלֵדוֹת*, *HALOT*), "generation."
פֶּרֶץ	See 4:12.
הוֹלִיד	Hiph suff 3ms (יָלַד), "to beget, father."

חֶצְרוֹן　　　Npr, "Hezron."

4:19

וְחֶצְרוֹן הוֹלִיד אֶת־רָם וְרָם הוֹלִיד אֶת־עַמִּינָדָב׃

רָם　　　Npr, "Ram."
עַמִּינָדָב　　　Npr, "Aminadab."

4:20

וְעַמִּינָדָב הוֹלִיד אֶת־נַחְשׁוֹן וְנַחְשׁוֹן הוֹלִיד אֶת־שַׂלְמָה׃

נַחְשׁוֹן　　　Npr, "Nahshon."
שַׂלְמָה　　　Npr, "Salmah," either an alternative form or a corruption of Salmon (cf. v. 21).

4:21

וְשַׂלְמוֹן הוֹלִיד אֶת־בֹּעַז וּבֹעַז הוֹלִיד אֶת־עוֹבֵד׃

עוֹבֵד　　　Npr, "Obed."

4:22

וְעֹבֵד הוֹלִיד אֶת־יִשַׁי וְיִשַׁי הוֹלִיד אֶת־דָּוִד׃

יִשַׁי　　　Npr, "Jesse."
דָּוִד　　　Npr, "David."

APPENDICES

Translation

CHAPTER 1

1:1
In the days when the judges governed [lit. "judging of the judges"], there was a famine in the land; so a man from Bethlehem of Judah went to sojourn in the country of Moab – he, and his wife, and his two sons.

1:2
Now the name of the man [was] Elimelech, and the name of his wife [was] Naomi, and the name of his two sons [were] Mahlon and Chilion, Ephrathites from Bethlehem of Judah; and they went to the country of Moab and stayed there [lit. "and they were there"].

1:3
Then Elimelech, the husband of Naomi, died, so she herself was left and her two sons.

1:4
And they took for themselves Moabite women [as wives]. The name of the one [was] Orpah, and the name of the other [was] Ruth. And they lived there about ten years.

1:5
Then the two of them, Mahlon and Chilion, also died, so that the woman was bereft of [lit. "left from"] her two children and her husband.

1:6
Then she herself rose with her daughters-in-law, and she returned from the country of Moab, for she heard in the country of Moab that Yahweh had visited his people to give food to them.

1:7
And she went from the place where she was, and her two daughters-in-law with her, and they went on the way to return to the land of Judah.

1:8
And Naomi said to her two daughters-in-law, "Go, return each of you to the house of her mother. May Yahweh do kindness to you as you have done with the dead and with me."

1:9
"May Yahweh grant that you find rest, each of you in the house of her husband." Then she kissed them and they lifted their voice and wept.

1:10
Then they said to her, "Surely, will we return with you to your people."

TRANSLATION

1:11
But Naomi said, "Go, my daughters! Why should you go with me? Have I still sons in my womb that they might be husbands for you?"

1:12
"Return, my daughters. Go! I am too old for a husband. If I said I have [lit. "there is for me"] hope, even if I had a husband this night, and even if I should bear sons…"

1:13
"…would you wait, therefore, until they grow up? Would you, therefore, let yourselves be hindered from marriage [lit. "be hindered so that there will not be (for you) a husband"]? No, my daughters, for it is more bitter for me than for you, because the hand of Yahweh has gone forth against me."

1:14
Then they lifted their voice and wept again, and Orpah kissed her mother-in-law, but Ruth clung to her.

1:15
And she said, "See! Your sister-in-law has returned to her people and to her gods. Return after your sister-in-law."

1:16
But Ruth said, "Do not entreat me to forsake you [or]

to return from [following] after you; for wherever [lit. "to where"] you go, I will go, and wherever [lit. "within where"] you live, I will live. Your people [will be] my people, and your God [will be] my God."

1:17
"Where you die, I will die, and there I will be buried. May Yahweh do thus to me and may he do thus worse [lit. "do again"], if [anything but] death divides between me and between you."

1:18
When she saw that she was determined to go with her, she ceased from speaking to her.

1:19
And the two of them went to go to Bethlehem. And when they came to Bethlehem, all of the city murmured about them, and the women [lit. "they"] said, "Is this Naomi?"

1:20
And she said to them, "Do not call me 'Naomi.' Call me 'Mara,' for the Almighty has caused great bitterness for me."[9]

1:21
"I went full, but Yahweh has brought me back empty.

---

[9] The name "Naomi" means "pleasant," and "Mara" means "bitter."

Why do you call me 'Naomi,' since Yahweh has answered against me? Indeed, the Almighty has treated me badly."

1:22
So Naomi returned, and Ruth, the Moabitess, her daughter-in-law, who returned with her from the country of Moab; and they came to Bethlehem at the beginning of the harvest of barley.

CHAPTER 2

2:1
Now there [was] for Naomi a kinsman of her husband, a wealthy man [lit. "a man, strong of wealth"] of the clan of Elimelech, and his name was Boaz.

2:2
And Ruth the Moabitess said to Naomi, "Please let me go to the field and I will glean among the ears of grain behind him in whose sight I may find favor." And she said to her, "Go, my daughter."

2:3
So she went and she came and she gleaned in the field after the harvesters; and by chance it was [lit. "her fortune befell on"] the portion of the field of Boaz,

who [was] of the clan of Elimelech.

2:4
And, see, Boaz was coming from Bethlehem, and he said to the reapers, "May Yahweh be with you," and they said to him, "May Yahweh bless you."

2:5
And Boaz said to his servant, who was foreman over the reapers, "To whom does this young woman belong?"

2:6
And the servant, who was foreman over the reapers, answered and said, "She is a young woman, a Moabite, who has returned with Naomi from the country of Moab."

2:7
"And she said, 'Please let me glean and gather among the sheaves after the reapers.' So she came and stood from that time – the morning – even until just now, sitting [in] the house a little [while]."

2:8
Then Boaz said to Ruth, "Listen closely, my daughter. Do not go to glean in another field, and also do not pass on from this one; but you should stay thus with my maidservants."

2:9
"[Keep] your eyes on the field which they are harvesting, and go after them. Have I not charged the young men not to touch you? When you become thirsty, go to the vessels and drink from those with which the young men are drawing water."

2:10
Then she fell on her face and prostrated herself to the ground, and she said to him, "Why have I found favor in your sight that you should regard me, since I am a foreigner?"

2:11
And Boaz answered and said to her, "All that you have done with your mother-in-law after the death of her husband has been told fully to me, and [that] you forsook your father and your mother and the land of your birth and came to a people that you did not know previously."

2:12
"May Yahweh reward your work, and may your wages be full from Yahweh, the God of Israel, under whose wings you have come to seek refuge."

2:13
Then she said, "May I [continue to] find favor in your sight, my lord, because you have comforted me and because you have spoken kindly [lit. "the heart of"] to

your maidservant, although I myself am not as one of your maidservants."

2:14
And at meal-time, Boaz said to her, "Come here, and eat of the bread, and dip your morsel in the vinegar." So she sat beside the reapers, and he held out parched grain to her, and she ate and was satisfied and had some left over.

2:15
When she rose to glean, Boaz commanded his servants, saying, "Let her glean even among the sheaves, and do not rebuke her."

2:16
"And be sure to draw out for her [some grain] from the bundles and leave [it] so that she may gather; and do not rebuke her."

2:17
So she gleaned in the field until the evening. Then she beat out what she had gleaned, and it was about an ephah of barley.

2:18
And she lifted [it] and went to the city, and her mother-in-law saw what she had gleaned. Then she took [it] out and gave to her what remained after her satiety.

Translation

2:19
Then her mother-in-law said to her, "Where did you glean today and where did you work? May he who regarded you be blessed." So she told her mother-in-law with whom she had worked and said, "The name of the man with whom I worked today [is] Boaz."

2:20
Then Naomi said to her daughter-in-law, "May he be blessed of Yahweh, who has not abandoned his kindness to the living or the dead." And Naomi said to her, "The man [is] a relative [lit. "near"] to us. He [is] one of our kinsmen.

2:21
Then Ruth said to her mother-in-law, "And he also said to me, 'Keep close with my young men [lit. "with the young men who are mine"] until they complete all my harvest [lit. "until they complete all of the harvest which is mine"].'"

2:22
And Naomi said to Ruth, her daughter-in-law, "It [is] good, my daughter, that you go with his maidservants so that they [i.e., miscreants] will not fall upon you in another field."

2:23
So she stayed close by the maidservants of Boaz to glean until the completion of the harvest of the barley

and the harvest of the wheat. And she lived with her mother-in-law.

CHAPTER 3

3:1
Then Naomi, her mother-in-law, said to her, "My daughter, shall I not seek rest for you that it may be well for you?"

3:2
"And now [is] not Boaz our kinsman, whose maidservants you were with? See, he is winnowing barley at the threshing-floor tonight."

3:3
"So wash yourself and anoint yourself and put on your [best] clothes, and go down to the threshing-floor. Do not make yourself known to the man before he finishes eating and drinking."

3:4
"And it shall be, when he lies down, that you shall learn of the place where he lies. Then you shall go and uncover his feet and lie down, and he himself will tell you what you should do."

3:5
And she said to her, "All that you say [to me] I will do."

3:6
And she went down to the threshing floor, and she did according to all that her mother-in-law had charged her.

3:7
When Boaz had eaten and drunk and his heart was pleased, he went to lie down at the end of the heap of grain. Then she came in secrecy and uncovered his feet, and she lay down.

3:8
And it happened at midnight [lit. "half the night"] that the man was startled, and he turned, and see! A woman lay at his feet.

3:9
And he said, "Who are you?" And she said, "I [am] Ruth, your maidservant, so spread your garment over your maidservant, for you [are] a redeemer."

3:10
And he said, "May you be blessed by Yahweh, my daughter. [In] this, your latter kindness, you have done better than the first – not going after young men, whether poor or rich."

3:11
"And now, my daughter, do not fear. All that you ask [lit. "say"] I will do for you; for all of my people at the gate know that you [are] a worthy woman."

3:12
"And now, truly, I [am] a redeemer, but there [is] a redeemer nearer than me."

3:13
"Lodge tonight and in the morning if he will redeem you, good, let him redeem; but if he is not pleased to redeem you, then, as Yahweh lives, I myself will redeem you. Lie down until the morning."

3:14
So she lay down at his feet until the morning, then she rose before anyone could be recognized [lit. "a man recognized his friend"]. And he said, "Let it not be known that the woman came to the threshing-floor."

3:15
And he said, "Give [me] the cloak that [is] on you and hold onto it." So she held it, and he measured six [measures] of barley and set [them] with her. Then he went to the city."

3:16
And she went to her mother-in-law, and she said, "How are you, my daughter?" Then she reported to her all that the man had done for her.

3:17
And she said, "He gave me these six [measures] of barley, for he said, 'you shall not go emptily to your mother-in-law.'"

3:18
And she said, "Wait, my daughter, until you know how the matter turns out, for the man will not rest unless he brings the matter to an end today."

CHAPTER 4

4:1
And Boaz went up to the gate and sat there; and, see, the redeemer of whom Boaz had spoken [was] passing by; so he said, "Turn aside, sit here, friend." So he turned aside and sat.

4:2
Then he took ten men of the elders of the city, and he said, "Sit her." So they sat.

4:3
And he said to the redeemer, "Naomi, who has returned from the country of Moab, is selling a portion of the field which belonged to our brother, Elimelech."

4:4
"Now I myself thought I would disclose to you, saying, 'Acquire [it] in front of those who are sitting and in front of the elders of my people: if you will redeem [it], redeem [it]; but if you will not redeem [it], tell me so that I will know, for there is no one except you to redeem [it], and I [am] after you.'" And he [the redeemer] said, "I will redeem [it]."

4:5
And Boaz said, "On the day [that] you acquire the field from the hand of Naomi, you also acquire Ruth, the Moabitess, wife of the deceased, in order to raise the name of the dead [i.e., Mahlon; cf. v. 10] on behalf of his inheritance."

4:6
Then the redeemer said, "I am not able to redeem [Mahlon's estate] for myself, lest I bring my inheritance to ruin. Redeem [it] for yourself. You [may have] my right of redemption, for I am unable to redeem [it]."

4:7
Now this [was the custom] formerly in Israel regarding the redemption and regarding the exchange [of property]: to confirm any matter, a man removed his sandal, and gave [it] to his fellow. And this [was the manner of] attestation in Israel.

4:8
So the redeemer said to Boaz, "Buy [it] for yourself," and he removed his sandal.

4:9
Then Boaz said to the elders and all of the people, "You [are] witnesses this day that I have bought all that belonged to Elimelech and all which belonged to Chilion and Mahlon from the hand of Naomi."

4:10
"And I have also acquired for myself Ruth, the Moabitess, the wife of Mahlon, for my wife to raise the name of the deceased concerning his inheritance, so that the name of the deceased will not be cut off from his brothers nor from the gate of his [birth] place. You [are] witnesses this day."

4:11
And all of the people who were at the gate and the elders said, "[We are] witnesses. May Yahweh make the woman who is coming into your house like Rachel and like Leah, the two of whom built the house of Israel, and may you acquire wealth in Ephrathah and gain fame in Bethlehem."

4:12
"And may your house be like the house of Perez, whom Tamar bore to Judah, from the seed which Yahweh will give to you by this young woman."

4:13
So Boaz took Ruth, and she became his wife [lit. "she became for him for a wife"], and he went into her; and Yahweh gave her conception and she bore a son.

4:14
Then the women said to Naomi, "May Yahweh be blessed, who has not let you be without a redeemer this day, and may his name become renowned in Israel."

4:15
"And may he be for you a restorer of life and a sustainer of your old age; for your daughter-in-law, who loves you, who is better for you than seven sons, has given birth to him."

4:16
And Naomi took the child and placed him on her lap and became his nurse.

4:17
And the neighbor women gave him a name [lit. called/proclaimed for him a name], saying, "A son has been born to Naomi." And they named him Obed. He [was] the father of Jesse, the father of David.

4:18
Now these are the generations of Perez. Perez fathered Hezron.

Translation

4:19

And Hezron fathered Ram, and Ram fathered Amminadab.

4:20

And Amminadab fathered Nahshon, and Nahshon fathered Salmah.

4:21

And Salmah fathered Boaz, and Boaz fathered Obed.

4:22

And Obed fathered Jesse, and Jesse fathered David.

Abbreviations

*	hypothetical Hebrew form
1	first person
2	second person
3	third person
act	active
adj	adjective
abs	absolute
adv	adverb
adv inter	interrogative adverb
art	definite article
BDB	F. Brown, S. R. Driver, and C. A. Briggs, *A Hebrew and English Lexicon of the Old Testament* (Oxford: Clarendon, 1907; repr., 1996; Peabody, Mass.: Hendrickson)
con	construct
coh	cohortative
conj	conjunction
du	dual
f	feminine
g	gentilic
GBH	Paul Joüon, *A Grammar of*

	Biblical Hebrew (translated and revised by T. Muraoka; rev. English ed.; *SubBi* 27; Roma: Pontifico Istituto Biblico, 2006)
HALOT	L. Koehler, W. Baumgartner, and J. J. Stamm, *The Hebrew and Aramaic Lexicon of the Old Testament* (trans. M. E. J. Richardson; study ed.; Leiden: Brill, 2001)
Hiph	Hiphil
IBHS	Bruce K. Waltke and M. O'Connor, *An Introduction to Biblical Hebrew Syntax* (Winona Lake: Eisenbrauns, 1990)
impv	imperative
inf abs	infinitive absolute
inf con	infinitive construct
juss	jussive
lit.	literally
m	masculine
n	noun
Niph	Niphal
p	plural
pass	passive
per	personal
pr	proper
pref	prefixed conjugation (=

Abbreviations

	imperfect, *yiqtol*)
prep	preposition
pret	preterite (= imperfect *wāw* consecutive/conversive, *wayyiqtol*)
pron	pronoun
pron dem	demonstrative pronoun
pron ip	independent personal pronoun
pron inter	interrogative pronoun
pron rel	relative pronoun
ps	pronominal suffix
ptcl	particle
ptcl ent	particle of entreaty
ptcl hyp	hypothetical particle
ptcl interrog	interrogative particle
ptcl neg	particle of negation
ptcp	participle
s	singular
suff	suffixed conjugation (= perfect, *qātal*)
s.v.	under the word
w/c	*wāw* consecutive
כ	Kethiv
ק	Qere

ACCENTS

The standard text of the Hebrew Bible that we generally use is that of *Codex Leningradensis* as appears in *Biblia Hebraica Stuttgartensia*. *Codex Leningradensis* reflects the text that was received and edited by a group of Jewish scholars/scribes called the Masoretes (see Introducing Kethiv/Qere, 1:8). Among the work of the Masoretes was the addition of a system of accents and vowels. Accents told the reader which syllable of the word to stress, thus assisting with pronunciation, and whether a word was connected syntactically to the following word, thus helping to identify the semantic units of the verse. Although not routinely taught in a one-semester introduction to Hebrew, accents are very useful in the process of translation, especially for the beginning student. Of all the accents, one is especially important, namely, the *'aṯnāḥ*, which marks the major division of the line. The reader should have a complete idea upon reaching the *'aṯnāḥ*. Otherwise, one should return to the beginning of the verse and try again. Although not an accent per se, the *sŏp̄ pāsûq* (:) is regular in that, like the English period or full stop, it marks the end of the verse/line.

Reading Ruth

The Masoretes grouped accents according to whether they were conjunctive (joining one word with the next word) or disjunctive (separating a word from the following word). The following table lists the accents by name and character using *mēm* as an example letter.[10]

Disjunctive Accents			Conjunctive Accents		
מִ֑ם	*Sillûq*	דָּבָ֑ר	מ֣	*mûnāḥ*	דָּ֣בָר
מֽ	*'aṯnāḥ*	דָּבָֽר	מ֤	*mᵉhuppāk̠*	דָּ֤בָר
מ֒	*sᵉḡŏltā'*	דָּבָ֒ר	מ֨	*mĕrḵā'*	דָּ֨בָר
מ֓	*šalšèleṯ*	דָּבָ֓ר׀	מ֦	*mĕrḵā' kᵉpûlā*	דָּ֦בָר
מ֔	*zāqēp̠ parvum*	דָּבָ֔ר	מ֧	*dargā*	דָּ֧בָר
מ֕	*zāqēp̠ magnum*	דָּבָ֕ר	מ֥	*'azlā*	דָּ֥בָר
מ֗	*rᵉḇîa'*	דָּבָ֗ר	מ֩	*ṯᵉlîšā' parvum*	דָּבָ֩ר
מ֖	*ṭip̠ḥā'*	דָּבָ֖ר	מ֖	*galga*	דָּ֖בָר
מ֘	*Zarqā*	דָּבָ֘ר	מ֤	*măp̠lā*	וַיֵּצֵ֤א־נֹ֗חַ
מ֙	*pašṭā*	דָּבָ֙ר			
מ֚	*ĵᵉṯîḇ*	דָּבָ֚ר			
מ֛	*tᵉḇîr*	דָּבָ֛ר			
מ֜	*Gèreš*	דָּבָ֜ר			

---

[10] The Masoretes used a different scheme for Psalms, Proverbs, and Job.

Accents

֨	*Garšájim*	דָּ֞בָר
֡	*Pāzēr*	דָּ֡בָר
֟	*pāzēr magnum*	דָּ֟בָר

Disjunctive Accents (cont.)

֠	*t̛lîšā magnum*	דָּ֠בָר
֓	*t̛garmēh*	דָּ֓בָר׀

The text used in this book, a Unicode adaptation of *Biblia Hebraica Stuttgartensia*, does not supply accents, therefore I have added them manually. In certain cases in which the 'azlā and the paštā accents occur in the same word, the font does not permit addition of the 'azlā accent clearly. In such cases I have omitted the 'azlā, but kept the paštā. Such instances should present no difficulty to the translator.

Basic Grammatical Terms

Adjective	A word that modifies a noun or participle (A *large, wooden* house.)
Adverb	A word that modifies a verb (She ran *quickly*).
Article	A word that makes a noun definite (*the* city is populous) or indefinite (*a city is populous*). English has definite and indefinite articles, but Hebrew has only the definite.
Clause	A group of words that, at its minimum, has a subject and a predicate, or, more fully, a subject, verb, and object. In the following examples, the subject is underlined and the predicate is italicized. He *sat.* The prophet *delivered the word of the LORD.*

Dependent clause	A clause which is incomplete in meaning by itself, and thus relies on another clause (the main clause) to complete its meaning. There are many types of dependent clauses. *Conditional* clauses express real or unreal conditions, and are signaled through an "if . . . then" pattern, although the "then" is often omitted (e.g., 1:12). *Temporal* clauses have to do with time, and are usually initiated with "when" (e.g., 1:18; 2:9). *Parenthetical* clauses break the narrative flow to give supplementary information, and are typically introduced with "now" (e.g., 1:2). *Result* clauses give the consequence of the action of the main clause and are usually introduced with "that."
Direct object	A word(s) to which the action of the verb applies (He read *the book*).
Main clause	A clause which is independent. As with dependent clauses, there are various types of main clauses. In the book of Ruth, for

	example, there are simple declarative clauses, which express a fact (e.g., 1:1), and rhetorical clauses, in which the speaker asks a question the answer of which is already known (e.g., 1:11). The speaker thus asks it to emphasize a point.
Noun	A person, place, or thing (e.g., respectively, *Sam, Mumbai, desk*).
Noun clause	See 1:2.
Participle	A word that has elements of a noun and verb, and can thus be used either nominally or verbally (The warrior, *raising* a sword . . .).
Phrase	Two or more words without a verb (in the morning).
Predicate	A word(s) that makes a statement about the subject (The king *ruled the people wisely*).
Preposition	"A word used with a noun or pronoun to show place, position, time or method" (*in* the house; *from* the river).[11]

---

[11] Catherine Soanes, ed., *Paperback Oxford English Dictionary* (2nd ed.; Oxford: University Press, 2006).

Pronoun	A word that takes the place of a noun. There are different types of pronouns, e.g., personal ("he," "she," "it") and demonstrative ("this," "that").
Subject	A word(s) about which something is stated (*Moses* gave the law).
Verb	A word that expresses action about its subject (Abraham *looked* and *saw* a ram).

www.ingramcontent.com/pod-product-compliance
Lightning Source LLC
LaVergne TN
LVHW051656080426
835511LV00017B/2603